Feast on a Leaf

Praise for the Book

'*Feast on a Leaf* is more than just a cookbook; it's a heartfelt tribute to the culinary heritage of Kerala, beautifully presented and meticulously detailed. Arun's expertise and passion shine through in every page.'

VIKAS KHANNA

'This is as much a cookbook as it is a labour of love. Arun's background as a filmmaker means he could have spent his life doing no more than cooking the odd good meal and treating food as a hobby. But such are his passion and his commitment that nearly two decades ago he made food his life's work specialising in the flavours so lovingly created by his forefathers. So this book is the work of a man who came to food only out of love and a sense of heritage. He takes us deep into the cuisine of Kerala but makes it accessible to even the novice cook.'

VIR SANGHVI

'Step into the vibrant world of Onam sadhyas with this exquisite cookbook that celebrates the rich tradition and cultural heritage of Kerala. *Feast on a Leaf* is more than just a collection of recipes – it's a culinary voyage that brings the essence of Onam to your kitchen.

Chef Arun Kumar T.R., a maestro of Kerala cuisine, unveils the secrets behind the grand feast. Through stunning photographs and detailed instructions, this book guides you in creating an authentic sadhya experience right at home. From the intricate preparation of each dish to the stories behind them, every page is a testament to the love and labour that goes into this traditional banquet.

Whether you're a seasoned cook or someone who loves sadhyas but is unsure where to start, *Feast on a Leaf* is your ultimate guide. Discover the joy of preparing and sharing a meal that's not just food, but a celebration of culture and community.

Get ready to immerse yourself in the flavours, colours, and traditions of Kerala. Your culinary adventure awaits.'

SUJAN SARKAR

'I remember Arun so well from the time he was my official Kerala food supplier at Café Diva nearly fifteen years ago. The nuances, subtle flavours, the honesty is something which I will never forget. In the book I loved his recipes but more than that it is the stories and the anecdotes. You can smell the air, taste the food and almost become part of the excitement that is around you during Onam.'

RITU DALMIA

'Having known Chef Arun for years, I've witnessed his deep-rooted passion for the rich cuisine of the South, especially Kerala food. This book is a treasure, a complete encyclopaedia of sadhya offerings – detailed insights into the traditional sadhya meal, its diverse accompaniments and different styles of preparation.'

MANISH MEHROTRA

'Part memories of a childhood spent in a Nair tharavad in Central Kerala, part meticulously detailed recipes of all the dishes that go to make up an Onam sadhya, arguably Kerala's most famous export to the world of gastronomy, Chef Arun Kumar who wears the hats of a chef and a film-maker has now donned the headdress of an author who has brought alive not only the snake-boat races of Onam, but the food, culture and frenetic preparations for the iconic lunch served on this occasion. A vital read.'

MARRYAM RESHII

Feast on a Leaf

THE ONAM SADHYA COOKBOOK

ARUN KUMAR T.R.

Photographs by Dinesh Khanna

BLOOMSBURY

NEW DELHI • LONDON • OXFORD • NEW YORK • SYDNEY

BLOOMSBURY INDIA
Bloomsbury Publishing India Pvt. Ltd
Second Floor, LSC Building No. 4, DDA Complex, Pocket C - 6 & 7,
Vasant Kunj, New Delhi 110070

BLOOMSBURY, BLOOMSBURY INDIA and the Diana logo
are trademarks of Bloomsbury Publishing Plc

First published in India 2024
This edition published 2024

ISBN: PB: 978-93-56405-61-5; e-ISBN: 978-93-56405-62-2
2 4 6 8 10 9 7 5 3 1

Printed and bound in India by Thomson Press India Ltd

To the Thelakat and Vadekepat tharavads

and

Poonam, Arjun, Chrissy

Contents

Desserts

Payasams

Other Sadhya Desserts

Appendix 1

Appendix 2

1

Memories, Legends, Traditions

When your mother let you play with mud, you knew something special was round the corner. And to me, still not in double digits at that time, it meant looking forward to plenty of goodies being made in the kitchen, getting new clothes, foraging around for flowers, helping sprinkle cow-dung water – anything and everything except studying. It was festival time. And you never heard the daily refrain: 'Go do your homework'. Memories and images from that age are both vivid and hazy, the timelines are not linear, but there is a story.

We lived in a small colony in what was then considered the outskirts of Bangalore, and my father was in charge of the airport which belonged to Hindustan Aeronautics Limited (HAL). The house we lived in was fairly large, built on an 800 square yard plot. We had a fish pond, shaped like a big cashew nut, surrounded by a garden that, apart from a variety of flowers, had seasonal and perennial vegetables and fruits: many types of beans, brinjal, okra, gourds, pumpkin, cabbage, cauliflower, greens, lemon, guava, papaya, custard apple, mango and other local crops. And a couple of handymen to look after all of them.

A wheelbarrow full of red clay would be dropped off by the gardener in one corner of the garden. And that was the mud which our mother let us loose on. The mission was to make tall, lean pyramids, which was easier said than done. Too much water mixed with the clay made the pyramids slowly but surely flop down. Too little water resulted in them not holding together. I wasn't getting the proportion right whereas my siblings, all older than me, were far more successful. We needed to make two pyramids, and I generously let the artistry and competence of my siblings take precedence. Luckily, the pyramids were not the only things that had to be constructed. People, utensils, vegetables, fruits – anything that we saw around us could be replicated in clay. I was definitely better at making things other than pyramids since the shape did not matter as much as the imagination.

After a few hours of coaxing the clay to take on various shapes, the items were placed in an open area so they could be exposed to the sun for the next couple of days.

The mud having been put away, the next day involved dealing with cow dung. More precisely, mixing it in water. Luckily, this mixture was made by our house help, who had gone around the colony following cattle and collecting fresh cow dung. We would tag along, guffawing as the animals were coaxed to drop dung. What we had to do was sprinkle this cow-dung water all over the front yard, not just to settle the mud but also to form the base for the next activity: making a pookolam, a flower carpet.

This meant collecting flowers of different colours. My mother was in charge of this bit, while we would try convincing her to use the flowers that each one of us had collected individually. To keep us out of her hair, she let us make little carpets of our own in different parts of the yard. They had to be concentric circles of different colours starting from a single dot. Not a successful activity for me as the circles I tried making turned out to be oblong, or worse. To add to this, it was done very early in the morning; not the best time for droopy eyes. And this activity was repeated every morning, with fresh flowers being added and the circle becoming bigger and bigger. Somewhere in between, on one of the days, our sculptures were placed in and around the main flower carpet.

The exciting part of these days – ten in all, as I now recall – was the food, especially the sweets that were prepared daily, culminating in a grand spread on the tenth day, the sadhya. Prior to this my mother would be frenetically busy in the kitchen with her sisters and some household helps, cutting a variety of vegetables, and grating and grinding coconuts.

If we were lucky, we were allowed to peel some of the vegetables and try our hand at cutting them, basically to keep us busy and not disturb the main action and to make us feel important.

On the final day, the living and dining rooms were emptied of all furniture. At lunchtime banana leaves were laid out, an activity in which we were allowed to participate. I was always corrected when I placed a leaf the wrong way. It took me years to realise that the tail of the leaf, the narrow portion, had to be on the left of the person eating off it.

It seemed like an open house for lunch. What I remember is that the children, along with the elderly, were served in the first round. Food just kept coming, and was served on various parts of the leaf. Salt at one end and payasam at the other. My first thought would be: is that all the payasam one was going to get? Before I could get a lick of it, innumerable items would be put on the leaf, with rice coming last, followed by a ladle full of sambar poured on top of it. This led to a battle on the leaf; one had to create a dam to stop the sambar from flowing all over. Those early images of the sadhya food are a blur. The important bit was that the kids were served payasam at the end of the meal in stainless steel glasses, and we could get as many helpings as we wanted. And there was leftover payasam which we got at night for dinner too.

Along with these early memories of celebrating the Onam festival, I have other mental images of these activities at my parents' tharavad houses in Kerala. We were lucky one year to have got permission to skip school and go to Kerala during Onam. The festivities were already on. A massive flower carpet. Grain newly harvested, in a big pile. Fresh vegetables hanging from the roof. Song and dance in the courtyard. Swings set up. We were in time for the big feast on the leaf to happen a few days later.

We children ran all over, playing hide and seek in the extremely large tharavad, careful not to venture too deep, as we feared we'd get lost and not be found for days, thus missing all the fun. So we kept all the hiding and seeking within a close perimeter of where the grown-ups were.

In the evening, we huddled as close as possible to the adults given that there was no electricity, and dealing with dark, elongated shadows created by the petromax and wick lamps was not very pleasant or comforting.

The ten days of Onam are:

Atham	Thrikketta
Chithira	Moolam
Chodhi	Pooradam
Vishakam	Uthradam
Anizham	Thiruvonam

The great-grandmother, looking both imposing and childish in a high chair with her impish smiles, kept us occupied with stories about Onam that seemed frightening as they involved a demon, Mahabali. But this demon was a good one, so we were comforted to an extent. The celebrations were connected to him. As children we did not think his coming from the netherworld to earth was a good idea, but the festivities associated with this visit were enjoyable. The story narrated involved the demon, the gods, some sort of a challenge and, as always, a boon and a happy ending. The details are again very blurry. My only memory is of finishing dinner quickly and rushing to bed hoping light would break soon.

While at home my mother was the leading force, at the maternal tharavad it was my great-grandmother, with my mother and aunts at her beck and call. She sat in her high chair supervising a dozen helps in the house. Us kids were not allowed to go into the kitchen but we did manage a few peeks. We saw women involved in many activities. Vegetables lying all over. Large brass pots on wooden fires with a couple of men stirring their contents. Women cutting vegetables, grinding coconuts. The great-grandmother giving instructions.

What I remember from home as being a large gathering was multiplied many times over in the tharavad. The great-grandmother distributed new clothes, along with grain and vegetables, to dozens of people who worked in the family's rice fields and orchards and at home. The children also got new clothes to be worn on the big day after a bath in the pond. The food on the leaf, and the battle on it, was similar, and so was the frenzy in the service. And yes, the children got payasam in glasses – not one but four different kinds.

But there was more to Onam and the Onam sadhya, the feast on a leaf, than what we absorbed as children.

Many, many Onams and sadhyas later, talking to some of the elders who remembered the goings-on at our tharavads, I learnt that each of the ten days of the Onam celebrations had a certain activity associated with it, even though the significance of each day varied in small details from tharavad to tharavad.

Day One

Atham is the first day of festivities in the ten-day-long Onam festival. Atham rituals involve an early-morning bath, prayers at the local temple and the making of the pookolam, an activity that continues for all ten days. There is a set breakfast of steamed bananas and fried pappadums. This breakfast is had on all ten days.

Day Two

Chithira is the second day of Onam festivities. It involves the customary temple visit and the laying of a fresh pookolam, as well as planning for the sadhya on the tenth day and buying new clothes. The shopping for the next day has to be planned in advance in the days of the tharavad as a dedicated person would have to travel to the nearest city to make the purchases.

Day Three

The third day is called Chothi or Chodhi. This is the day for shopping for new clothes. More flowers are added to the fresh pookolam, which becomes even larger. In fact, different types of flowers are added to the pookolam on each day as each flower is devoted to a particular deity.

Day Four

Vishagam or Visakam is the fourth day. On this day apart from the visit to the temple and the laying of a fresh pookolam, preparations for the sadhya continue.

Day Five

Anizham is the fifth day. Traditionally, it is the day for Vallam Kali (water sports), the day when boat races are held on the backwaters.

Day Six

Triketta or Thriketa is the sixth day. While there are no specific rituals for this day, it marks the homecoming for people staying away from their families.

Day Seven

The seventh day is Moolam. By now the tharavads are full, with most family members having arrived. So it is time for fun and games. Singing and dancing mark this day, while other activities like the pookolam and sadhya preparations continue, with many more hands to help.

Day Eight

Pooradam is the eighth day. This is the day of the Onathappans, the clay pyramids we children enjoy making. It is also the day for families and friends to visit each other.

Day Nine

Utradam or Uthradam is the ninth and penultimate day of the festival of Onam. Some people also call Utradam the first Onam and the next day, Thiruvonam, as the second Onam. On the day of Utradam tenants and dependants of Nair Tharavads bring the produce of their farms to the Karanavar (eldest maternal uncle of the tharavad or the eldest member with authority). These gifts from the tenants to the Karanavar are called Onakazhcha. In the tharavads, the Karanavar is seated in the verandah to greet people. They are treated with a sumptuous meal, a sadhya, and gifted with new clothes.

Day Ten

Thiruvonam Aashamsakal! The greeting, which means 'To everyone, Onam Wishes', is the common refrain of the day. The Onathappans are placed alongside the pookolam and worshipped. As per the popular legend, this is the day Mahabali visits his people. The Onam sadhya is at noon. It is largely a family affair, with each home or tharavad having its own sadhya.

Some rituals are also marked for the eleventh and twelfth days, called Avittom and Chatayam or Chathayam, respectively. But the major celebrations get over on the tenth and most important day of Thiruvonam.

2

Looking for Onam

After the COVID-19 pandemic, people suddenly realised the vulnerability of life and began getting nostalgic, seeking refuge in memories of good times. Even I embarked on a journey to Kerala looking for the Onam of my childhood and seeking the tale of its origin.

How is Onam celebrated in Kerala today? Is it what it once was, a ten-day celebration with each day marked for a specific activity? What does it mean for the people of Kerala?

The first thing I decided to explore was the legend of Onam. How and when did the Vishnu–Mahabali tale become associated with Onam? There are no historical texts that either validate the tale or pinpoint the origin of the festival. Associating it with the harvest and nature's renewal after the monsoon seems logical, but then what is a festival without legend or folklore?

According to folklore, once upon a time, there was a king named Mahabali (also referred to as Raja Bali or Maveli) who ruled over the ancient land of Kerala. Mahabali is often depicted as a demon king in Hindu mythology, but his character is not entirely negative. He is known for his wisdom, generosity and fairness, and is greatly loved by his people.

The gods were worried about Mahabali because he had become too powerful and popular among the people. They feared losing their status and power. Moreover, the people were so content and happy under Mahabali's rule that they had stopped worshipping the gods, which caused a decline in the latter's powers. Therefore, the gods turned to Vishnu for help. He took on the form of a dwarf named Vamana to trick Mahabali and regain power for them.

Vishnu, in the form of Vamana, approached Mahabali and asked for a small piece of land that he could call his own. Mahabali, known for his generosity, agreed to the request and asked Vamana to specify the size of the land he wanted with his feet. Three, said Vamana. Vamana then revealed his true form as Vishnu and grew in size until he was large enough to cover the entire earth with one foot and all of heaven with the other. He then asked Mahabali where he should place his third foot. Mahabali, recognising Vishnu, offered his own head for the third footstep. Vishnu then placed his foot on Mahabali's head and pushed him into the netherworld. However, Mahabali's spirit was so pure that Vishnu granted him immortality and allowed him to return to his kingdom once a year during the festival of Onam.

Now this is the popular folklore. Is that what Onam is all about?

Venugopal Paliath considers Onam a harvest festival and more of a Vishnu pooja and feels it has little to do with the myth of Mahabali's return. Venugopal manages the Paliam Trusts of the Paliam family based at Chendamangalam in the Ernakulam district of Kerala with an antiquity of no less than a thousand years. He is well-versed with his family's history and the scriptures. The folklore, he feels, is a misinterpretation of the scriptures.

'The popular folklore talks about Mahabali being pushed down to Patal Lok and returning every year to visit his people. That's not correct. Vamana Avatar, the avatar Vishnu took, is the main thing. The story has been described very beautifully in Bhagavatam. Raja Bali, not any Mahabali, was an asura king and a stage came when he controlled almost the entire universe and had surrounded Amravati, the celestial city of Lord Indra. Indra was afraid he may lose his throne. Raja Bali was doing a very big yagya, after which he would become Chakravarti. To avoid this, Indra sought the help of Vishnu. Vishnu took on the avatar of

Vamana, a small Brahmin dwarf and came begging for alms. Raja Bali was known for his generosity, and seeing a puny Brahmin allowed Vamana to ask for anything. Raja Bali's Kula Guru, Shukracharya, tried to warn him against such a promise but Raja Bali's ego got the better of him and he told Vamana to ask for anything. And then you know the rest, but according to the Bhagavatam, Vishnu did not push him to Patal Lok but to Sutal Lok, and there is no mention of Vishnu letting Mahabali return every year.

'Onam day is simply Vamana Jayanti. That is what our family has always followed. It is the birth of Vamana, the avatar Vishnu took to address Indra's concerns.'

Venugopal Paliath is correct going by some of the accepted interpretations of the Bhagavatam. In his book *Discourses on Shrimad Bhagavata*, Swami Tejomayananda interprets the Raja Bali incident describing Vishnu when he assumed his cosmic form:

> Lord Vamana's form became so huge that his one step covered the entire earth and His next step covered all of heaven (Swarg Lok) ... The Lord's third step still remained ... The Lord said to Bali, My first step measured the earth in full and my second covered the heavens. Tell Me, where should I place the third step? Your promise has not yet been fulfilled and if it remains so, you will incur sin ...
>
> Raja Bali, in response, said:
>
> O Lord, if You think I have lied, it is not so. I will fulfil my promise so that I do not incur sin. My head is before You. Please place Your foot on my head as Your third step.

Swami Tejomayananda further interprets how the Lord was impressed with Raja Bali:

> The Lord said to Bali: I will place My foot on your head and you will go straight to Sutal Lok. This realm offers great bliss, greater than even heaven. There you will rule as king. You will eternally find Me there. I will stand at your palace gates forever with My discus, mace, conch and lotus in hand, to serve as your guard and gatekeeper.[1]
>
> The Bhagavatam has no mention of Lord Vishnu granting any other boon, like allowing Raja Bali to return to earth to meet his people.

Radha Thampuran, my maternal aunt, who is married into the Kochi royal family, reiterates Venugopal Paliath's thought that the erstwhile royal family worshipped Vishnu for Onam, and that the return of Mahabali and his worship is a recent, popular phenomenon. For the erstwhile maharaja of Kochi, the high point of his Onam celebration was visiting the Thrikkakkara temple to worship Vishnu.

So when did the return of Mahabali folklore become the central point of Onam celebrations? While this legend was gaining popularity among the people in Kerala, it was in the sixties that the communist government declared Onam a state festival revolving around the popular Mahabali legend. It is a folktale that gradually appealed to the public imagination (like it fascinated us as children when it was narrated by our great-grandmother) and the government was able to take advantage of this and make the festival less religious and more celebratory so that it encompassed all the people of Kerala.

Devika, a feminist researcher and social scientist, traces this transformation of Onam from a religious festival to a more inclusive one in an article for Kafila:

> Onam was actually declared the 'national festival' of Kerala only in 1960, and in the decades immediately preceding we had witnessed an important transformation in its meaning, in what it represented. Onam used to be, in many parts of Kerala, actually more a celebration of Vishnu, rather than Maveli, and domestic rituals associated with Onam celebrated not Maveli but Vamanamurty (Vishnu's Vamana avatar). However, a different interpretation of Onam was forged in precisely the decades in which the movement for uniting Malayalam-speaking regions into Kerala gathered force, one in which the Left was certainly a hegemonic presence.
>
> Onam came to be reinterpreted as the festival celebrating the benevolent asura king Maveli, his yearly return from exile, and Vamana receded in importance – especially in some of the most brilliant poetry produced in Malayalam in the 1940s and 1950s. Maveli and the modern welfare state came to mirror each other. School textbooks have since then spread the story of Mahabali and of Onam as the occasion for remembering him, made it part of popular understanding.[2]

Reminiscing about Onam she told me, 'For my family, as far as I remember, it's about Maveli coming, and Vamana was definitely not celebrated anywhere in my memory.

---

[1] Swamin Tejomayananda, Discourses on Shrimad Bhagavata (Chinmaya Prakashan, 2022), Canto 8, Chapter 11.

[2] J. Devika, 'Happy Onam, [Kallu] Shaappy Onam!', *Kaafila*, 9 September 2011.

'Onam was never religious. I mean, in the sense, it was a celebration of a harvest and the centre of the celebration was always the Onathappan [the clay pyramid representing Mahabali], never Maha Vishnu.

'Yes, in central Kerala they worshipped Maha Vishnu. Over the years this has changed too, except in a few families perhaps that continue to worship Maha Vishnu.'

In fact, I noticed this change at my aunt's house, located in Tripunithura in central Kerala, where my cousins demonstrated some of the key elements of the festival for me as I sought out what Onam signifies in today's Kerala.

After putting together a pookolam, they brought out the Onathappans they had made: two large ones and a small one. One of the large pyramids and the small one were placed at the head of the pookolam. The other large Onathappan was placed at the gate of the house. A lamp was lit near the pookolam. One cousin went to the Onathappan at the gate with some flowers and a white liquid (rice flour in water). She sprinkled some of the liquid on it and then traced a line from there to the pookolam, then up to the entrance of the house. This, I was told, was symbolic of inviting Mahabali to visit the house. The little Onathappan was the Vamana avatar of Vishnu.

There is no doubt that Mahabali is now the focus of Onam. Today, when you go to Kerala during Onam, you see Mahabali everywhere: on posters announcing a sale, as a cutout at the entrance to a shop and as men dressed like him at malls, hotels and restaurants, greeting people. Interestingly, the symbol of the umbrella carried by the Vamana avatar has passed on to Mahabali.

For my cousin Latha, the smell of sambar being made a day before Onam was a highlight. 'So striking was the smell of sambar being made by our cook, Narayan Nair. There was something special about his sambar. Apart from that there would be a lot happening. There would be a fire pit outside where the cooking was done. There would be the ada (rice flakes) being made, vegetables being cut. A lot of activity and I loved being around it all.

'When I was at home it also meant that first thing in the morning you make the pookolam for ten days. That was like a must. But when I got married and moved away from home, that kind of dropped off. I was busy with the kids. The whole concept of [making the] pookolam every day kind of dropped off, though Amma would send us wooden madheras, the Onathappans, which we would put and do a little pookolam on the day of Onam.'

Another cousin of mine, Jayashree, is one of those who still tries to do as her parents and grandparents did at their tharavad, but on a smaller scale. She spearheads the celebration my aunt simulates for me. While laying the pookolam she talks about the flowers she picked during her childhood from the tharavad gardens, which she says cannot be found now. They have been replaced by flowers imported from the neighbouring state of Tamil Nadu.

'We were around ten kids. Every day we would run around the garden collecting these very colourful flowers. A fresh pookolam was made every morning for ten days. It would be round for the first nine days and then on the tenth day it would be square. I remember we had ten days of holidays, so it was a lot of fun. Today the elders are no more and the family is scattered. We try but we hardly do as much as we have seen earlier.

My aunt Radha Thampuran, who helped me look for the 'lost Onam' of our childhood, went abroad soon after marriage. On returning many, many years later she did revive some of the old customs and rituals for some time but with her growing children to look after, and them getting married and going abroad, she confined the celebrations to just the sadhya and a small pookolam on Onam day. However, she has made it a point to gift her house helps with new clothes and some money every Onam.

The customs and rituals of the past are fast disappearing because the whole concept of a joint family and a tharavad no longer exists. Members of a family are invariably spread across the globe.

Venugopal Paliath, talking about the large Paliam family and the tharavad homes in Chendamangalam in Ernakulam district, laments, 'Here we still have the tharavad houses. Part of it is a museum. Others are either locked or have very elderly people staying. The younger ones have all gone to various cities and countries. So for Onam these tharavads have no celebration. The old ways of life in these tharavads no longer exist. Onam for them is just another day.'

For Devika, the memories are not so much of the rituals but nature itself and, of course, the food.

'The good thing about Onam is that it's also something that inevitably comes every year. Something that you can expect. And in a rural setting, it used to be a very beautiful rural festival with a lot of nature in it. It was also a celebration of nature in the sense that after the rains, after the two, three months of incessant rain you had this beautiful clearing, of lovely sun. And the sun in August was very special in Kerala. And that's also the time when all the tiny insects and everything was breeding. The air was full of dragonflies and butterflies and all kinds of teeny-weeny creatures. There was life thriving everywhere.

'In my father's house, which was a very large farm, my father's sisters would be making all kinds of special eats. Tapioca chips, banana chips, murukku (a twisted savoury, crunchy snack), ellu unda (sweet sesame ball), ari unda (sweet rice flour ball) ... there would be these biscuit tins full of these. It was non-stop eating. Morning to night you are munching something.

'Of course, there were a lot of collective things happening. For us kids, the advantage was that none of my aunts worked professionally, so they would work at home. They were able to give us this experience of unending amounts of treats and food and attention and whatnot.' Over the years, the Kerala state government has been promoting and holding extravagant cultural programmes across the state.

In olden days, the maharaja of Kochi used to conduct the festival and special poojas at Thrikkakkara Vamanamurty temple on Atham, the first day of Onam. Athachamayam was the procession led by the maharaja from Tripunithura to the Vamana temple at Thrikkakkara. It was an occasion to show off regal pomp as well as to herald Onam.

Representatives from all communities accompanied the maharaja during the procession. These included a priest from the Karingachira church, the head priest of the Nettur Thangal mosque, and Chembil Arayan, a representative of the fisher folk.

It was a day when everyone, irrespective of caste and creed, was allowed to enter the Kottakkakam (fort). In 1948 the last Athachamayam led by royalty was held during the reign of Rama Varma (Pareekshith Thampuran). When Kochi state merged with the Indian Union, there ceased to be an Athachamayam procession.

In the early 1960s, along with the efforts of the government to make Onam a state festival, the people of Tripunithura decided to revive it. Athachamayam was renamed Athaghosham.

Since the formation of the Tripunithura Municipal Council in 1980 and the participation of the state government along with folk artists from across the state, Athaghosham is now the new Athachamayam. It involves the participation of people from all walks of life and once again it marks the beginning of the ten-day festival of Onam.

Retaining the involvement of royalty, on the evening before Athachamayam, there is a ceremonial flag handover at the Hill Palace by descendants of the erstwhile maharaja of Kochi to the local authorities. This flag, known as the Atham flag, is hoisted the next day at the Boys' Higher Secondary School in Tripunithura to mark the beginning of the celebrations.

My quest to find out more about Onam led me to the school grounds on a Sunday. Given the natural disasters and pandemic in the recent years, at this Athachamayam one could sense an increased enthusiasm. The school grounds started filling up early in the morning. The stage came alive with innumerable announcements being made regarding Athachamayam, its history and significance. A large, hangar-like space had been converted into a huge green room. There were hundreds of people in various costumes getting last-minute touch-ups, and an equal number of onlookers milling around clicking photographs. There were the unmistakable Pulikali dancers with their bodies painted in the stripes and colours of tigers and wild cats, the striking Theyyam and Kathakali dancers with intricately painted faces, sporting enormous head-dresses, and a pantheon of gods and goddesses, all in bright costumes, seated on decorated palanquins. There were groups of women in the trademark Kerala dress – mundus with bright borders – practising their Kaikottikali skills. Accompanying all these sights were the percussion and wind-pipe sounds from Panchavadhyam and Chenda Melam groups rehearsing their beats.

In another part of the ground hundreds of schoolchildren of various age groups representing schools from across the district were lining up. There were dozens of school bands, each rehearsing tunes. There were children in costumes depicting characters from epics, some in traditional attire carrying thalis with lamps, some in school uniforms holding placards with social messages – all eagerly awaiting their turn and place in the Athachamayam procession.

The stage came alive with the arrival of a couple of Mahabalis. The crowds cheered. The Mahabalis descended and moved among the crowds. Some people in the crowd went into an obeisance pose while others jostled to get selfies with them.

The year I went the chief minister was there to light the ceremonial lamp and flag off the celebrations. He was accompanied by the Malayalam movie star Mammootty. After the flag hoisting and the lighting of the lamp, a colourful parade was taken out in the narrow streets of Tripunithura town, led by the many people dressed as Mahabali.

The procession was massive and consisted of folk dancers from across Kerala, schoolchildren's bands, dances, acrobatics and innumerable floats of government departments highlighting their achievements, floats of private companies and groups promoting social awareness messages. This cavalcade, which was about a kilometre long, travelled around the city before returning to the start point. It took a couple of hours.

This was an occasion to witness almost all folk-art forms of the state: Theyyam, Kolkali, Mayilattam, Kummi, Pulikali, Kathakali, Panchavadhyam, Chenda Melam, and many more which are displayed in the parade. This Athachamayam procession also kicks off a host of activities in town for the ten days of Onam. By evening the school grounds had turned into a huge carnival; there were innumerable exciting rides for children, a 'well of death' with long queues of people eager to watch the daredevil in it, eating stalls offering a variety of snacks and kiosks selling local products.

At a hall nearby a pookolam competition was being held, where groups of people young and old put together the most intricate flower designs. What was once a simple flower carpet enthusiastically put together by children at home was transformed into a very intricate activity involving the use of geometry sets and creation of designs with a 3-D effect.

On every evening of the Onam celebrations, dance programmes, music recitals, magic and puppet shows are held across the city. One of the popular performances is the Kaikottikali, an integral part of Onam, which now involves professional dancing groups instead of young girls in tharavads. From the tharavad compounds the dance has moved to the city square.

Vallam Kali, or water sports, continues to be a popular Onam activity, especially on the backwaters. What was earlier a friendly canoe-racing event during Onam between neighbouring villages has now become a major sporting event. The highlight is the iconic Chundan Vallam, which translates to 'snake boat' in English. These long and narrow boats can extend up to a hundred feet in length and are manned by a large crew. The design of the boat resembles a snake with its raised hood, and it requires skilful rowing and coordination.

Apart from Chundan Vallam, there are several other categories of boats that participate in the races, each with its own unique design and rowing style. Some of the other popular categories include Iruttukuthy Vallam, Odi Vallam and Veppu Vallam.These days professional boat races are organised at various locations across Kerala, with the most famous one being the Nehru Trophy Boat Race held on the Punnamada Lake near Alappuzha. Other notable venues include the Ashtamudi Lake and the Pamba River.

The participating teams engage in rigorous training and practice sessions leading up to the races. The rowers follow a synchronised rhythm, and each team aims for perfect coordination to achieve maximum speed. I was lucky to witness one of these races just outside Kochi in Aroor district. As we approached the backwater stretch on which the races were going to be held, we went past hundreds of people hastening towards the spot, not wanting to miss out on the action. Along the backwaters, on a sandy stretch, a big shamiana had been erected with seating arrangements. There was hardly an empty chair to be found.

Dozens of trophies were lined up on a table, and announcements of participants, sponsors and well-wishers were being made.

We decided to stay on the bridge over the backwaters as from there we could get a bird's eye view of the entire racing stretch. Hundreds of people were already thronging the bridge. It was difficult finding a good view, not so much because of the people but the umbrellas they carried.

Malayalees are very fond of their umbrellas. The sun has to be barely visible and umbrellas will be opened. It needs to just about drizzle and the umbrellas will be up. And if nothing else, one hand is always occupied holding an umbrella. It is almost an extension of most Malayalees.

Gently pushing aside open umbrellas, I could see four lanes marked on the backwaters with the help of buoys. There were small and large boats carrying spectators floating around the finish lane. Hundreds of metres away the boats participating in the race were lined up. These were medium-sized boats with around thirty to forty oarsmen. An announcement and a commentary spiel began as the race started. I could see splashes of water alongside the boats in unison, and as they approached the finish line, a Panchavadhyam troupe got into action. The commentator was shouting ecstatically, the percussion tempo had reached a crescendo as the boats crossed the finish line, and a loud cheer went up. The excitement of the people was to be heard and seen to be believed. It went on for nearly two hours, getting closer to sunset, as the victorious teams and individuals collected prizes and awards. The boat races were followed by a lot of singing and dancing.

The celebrations are no longer confined to the large compounds of tharavad houses; now the whole city is part of the ten-day carnival. And the icing on this celebration which involves shopping, alcohol, cultural extravaganzas and sporting activities is the government-promoted bumper lottery, with prize money running into crores (and increasing year by year). The lottery has now become an integral part of Onam. If money is not spent on shopping or alcohol, it is spent on lottery tickets. At every nook and corner, you will be flashed with lottery tickets. It is difficult resisting the urge to buy one and hope for the bumper prize.

I needed just a little persuasion by my taxi driver Abdul to be tempted and buy a ticket. He regaled me with stories of how people would get together and buy a large number of lottery tickets, like a community activity, to increase the chances of winning and sharing the prize money. He also told me that past winners were invariably from the middle and lower middle class.

I partnered with Abdul to buy a couple of tickets. All that I am left with now are pieces of paper promising the moon and more! They will always remind me of Onam.

Apart from the hope he got from the lottery tickets Abdul was looking forward to one more thing: the Onam sadhya, which Onam has become synonymous with. Today, this feast on a leaf comes out of modern kitchens, not out of unique tharavad cooking areas where practices that were in tune with nature were followed.

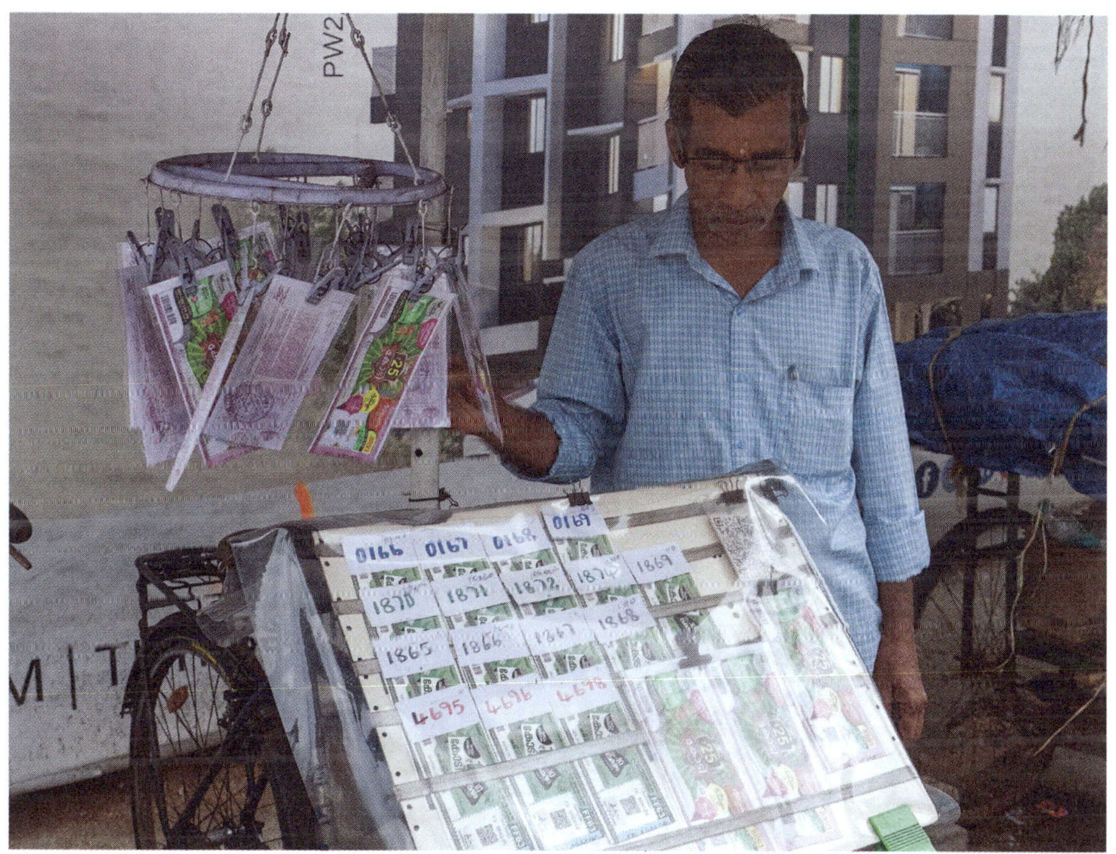

3

Ammis, Urulis, Chattis

The two tharavad houses where we spent our holidays as children were ideal for us to play hide and seek, but the fear was always that we would never be found! There were innumerable rooms in these houses – some never-used, dark corners that hadn't ever seen the light of day. Two areas were always forbidden, and hence both tempting and daunting: the upstairs and the kitchen.

The upstairs, where we usually slept, had many rooms with heavy, creaking wooden doors, large paintings on the walls and almirahs full of curios and books. We were not allowed to go upstairs unless accompanied by an adult. As we climbed up, the wooden stairs would creak and the almirahs rattle with the vibrations created by our footsteps. At night going upstairs was like walking on to the sets of a horror film. Apart from the sound effects, the lanterns we carried created visual effects befitting a movie with ghosts. Our shadows danced to a tune of their own and brought to life the paintings on the wall!

The other no-go area was a very tempting one, but the adults had declared it a 'danger zone': the kitchen. In a tharavad house, the kitchen was more than just a functional cooking space; it was a place where the family's culinary heritage was preserved and passed down through generations. It played a central role in family gatherings, as well as in religious and cultural rituals. The design and elements of the kitchen were rooted in Kerala's traditional lifestyle and culinary traditions, making it an integral part of a tharavad house's cultural identity.

The kitchen served as a social space where the family gathered and shared stories. Cooking was often a collaborative effort, with different family members contributing to the preparation of meals. Elders in the family passed down traditional recipes and cooking techniques to younger generations.

I describe them in the past tense as it is rare to find a traditional tharavad house now, let alone one with such a kitchen. Many of the few that remain are converted into homestays and museums, which entail a lot of modernisations and retain only the basic structure. A few of them are under dispute and extremely rundown. In fact, even with the introduction of electricity – which I witnessed in one of our tharavads – something was taken away. The living areas were lit with tube lights which enveloped the space with a dead look. The kitchens went from using firewood to gas, necessitating the introduction of cooking counters. It is in a way selfish to expect the owners of these tharavads to 'live in the past'. But it is still possible for some of the old practices and workflow followed in these kitchens to be retained.

Typically, the kitchen in a tharavad house was located adjacent to the central courtyard, the nadumuttom, or in close proximity to the other living areas, making it a central part of the household. This placement facilitated easy access to the kitchen from various parts of the house. These traditional Kerala kitchens were characterised by their simple and functional design. They usually had an open layout, allowing for proper ventilation and natural light. The kitchen would have walls on three sides with an open side leading to the courtyard or a verandah.

The focal point of the kitchen was the wood-fired stove, the adupu, which was typically made of clay. Depending on space there would be two to four such stoves, designed to accommodate multiple cooking vessels simultaneously. A storehouse within or next to the kitchen had various traditional utensils and cookware, including heavy-bottomed iron or brass vessels, earthenware pots and coconut-shell ladles.

Some of the traditional vessels and implements one found here were:

- **Uruli:** a shallow, circular, bronze vessel in various sizes
- **Man chatti** or **chenna chatti:** clay pots of various sizes
- **Kal chatti:** stone pot
- **Charakku:** round bronze cauldron
- **Idli patharam:** brass steamer to make idlis
- **Kindi:** brass container with a spout for pouring water
- **Ada chatti:** cast-iron frying pan
- **Unniyappa chatti:** special iron pan for making unniyappams (sweet rice dumplings)
- **Chiratta puttu kutti:** coconut-shell puttu (cylindrical rice and coconut cakes) maker
- **Sevanazhi:** a press for making idiyappam (string hoppers)
- **Dosa kal:** iron pan for making dosas
- **Kadukuthali:** cast-iron seasoning pans, big and small
- **Ammi kal:** large granite stones used for grinding spices and other ingredients; one flat and the other hollow
- **Iddi kal:** stone or brass mortar and pestle of various sizes

These kitchens typically had a sloping roof made of terracotta or tiled sheets. The design helped in directing smoke and heat away from the cooking area, providing a more comfortable environment within the kitchen. There was adequate ventilation to remove odours and heat in the form of windows with intricate wooden latticework which not only allowed airflow but also maintained privacy. There was a dedicated grinding area which housed the grinding stones and the large stone mortar–pestle used for pounding grains. Apart from natural light seeping in during the day and the glow from the wood-fire flames, the lighting in the kitchen was typically provided by oil lamps or traditional brass and copper lamps.

The water source was a well adjacent to the kitchen. In our tharavads a wide opening along the side overlooked a well which had a pulley system with a bucket to facilitate the availability of fresh groundwater.

Just as hotels have an executive chef, our tharavads had two people who were in charge of the kitchens. At my maternal tharavad it was Shanguman, who not only cooked delicious meals but also helped in various other activities in the house. He was my maternal great-grandmother's right-hand man. Orders passed by her were transmitted to the relevant people and overseen by him. At my paternal tharavad the kitchen was run by Chinnammu, a very pleasant lady who went out of her way to accommodate our tastes. She was assisted by Raman Nair, my paternal grandmother's right-hand man.

Once a week, or every other day, depending on demand, the right-hand men would procure vegetables and fruits from the gardens or orchards. These would be spread out in front of the lady of the house, who sat on a high chair in the verandah. The produce would be sorted and after a discussion a decision would be taken about what would be cooked the next day and what would be stored.

Tharavad houses had dedicated areas where grains, fruits and other provisions were stored. They were designed to maintain a cool and dark environment, helping to preserve the freshness of stored items. Wooden storage boxes made from sturdy wood and with multiple compartments were commonly used to keep fruits and vegetables, allowing for an organised storage of different items. Hanging bamboo baskets were used to store fruits like bananas. These baskets were hung from the ceiling in well-ventilated areas, preventing the fruits from coming into contact with surfaces and promoting air circulation. Wooden racks and shelves were used to store fruits and vegetables that did not require complete darkness. The open design of these racks allowed air to circulate, preventing the growth of mould and keeping the items fresh. Palm leaf mats were often used to line shelves or trays where fruits were stored. They helped in maintaining a clean and dry surface, preventing fruits from rotting due to moisture.

Certain fruits were stored in earthenware or clay pots, which helped in maintaining cool temperatures. The pots were often covered with lids to protect the contents from dust and pests. Banana leaves were commonly used to wrap and store certain fruits, providing natural and biodegradable packaging. This method also helped protect fruits from insects and other environmental factors. Net bags or mesh bags were used to store onions and shallots, allowing air to circulate to prevent mould. These bags were often hung in well-ventilated areas of the kitchen or the storage room.

It's important to note that these traditional storage methods were not only practical but also aligned with what we emphasise today as sustainable and eco-friendly practices of the region. The natural materials used in storage, such as wood, bamboo, palm leaves, contributed to the overall ethos of living off and in harmony with the environment.

During vacations and festivals the tharavad kitchen came alive in all its glory, bursting at the seams as families from the cities descended on them. This meant many more mouths had to be fed. Apart from the normal meals, the kitchen also produced innumerable goodies, some consumed then and there and others packed and sent with the families returning to their urban homes. These goodies included a variety of chips, pickles, chakka varathi or jackfruit jam, adamanga – which are sweet, sour and pungent dried mango strips seasoned over months – rice and fruits, depending on the season. Large vessels were brought out of storage. The urulis were big enough to fill water and splash around in. The wooden ladles made excellent 'swords'; the metal ones we could not play around with as they were lethal.

The kitchen became active very early in the morning. Us children rarely saw the preparations but after we had brushed our teeth in the morning we would see that breakfast was ready. It would vary from idli to dosa to puttu or upma. There would be the mandatory coconut chutney and podi. When it was upma or puttu – not great favourites with us children – we would be given bananas to eat along with it. This made it more palatable. Bournvita, which was carried by our parents, was mixed with milk for the children. We avoided Horlicks, which remains a favourite in Kerala homes. The adults had coffee or tea, which was stored in large flasks.

By this time lunch preparations would have begun. On a normal day we would get sambar, another curry, a couple of thorans, pickles and pappadums. In our tharavads the staple was always rice; I do not remember chapatis being served. (Today, Kerala chapatis, that are prepared and stored in a casserole, are a staple along with rice.) The kitchen was thoroughly cleaned after lunch. The evening offerings from the kitchen were always exciting. On the sweet side there would be unniyappam, pazham pori, ela ada, halwa and coconut burfis and on the savoury side murukku, chips and pakoras. Our grandmothers made sure the children were offered the largest variety possible during tea. Dinner was light, usually just a curry and a thoran with accompaniments. Many of the adults just had kanji – rice gruel with pappadum – kondattum or fried bitter gourd and pickle. Our appetites at dinner were never great given all that we'd eaten at teatime.

At times we sneaked into the kitchen to try our hands at lighting the wood-fire by blowing at embers through a hollow metal tube. We only ended up inhaling smoke and filling the whole kitchen with it, sending everyone into coughing bouts. This coughing was like an alarm, alerting the adults, and so we would scurry away. Other times, when no alarms would be set off, we would get a chance to stir what was cooking. It made us feel as if we had made the dish. That gentle stirring, steam emanating from the curry, mixing with the smoke from the fire and creating unique smells was most alluring. It was perhaps then that I decided what I wanted to be.

What was always very tempting to have a go at but we were never allowed to use was the meen chatti, the fish-shaped, curved cutting board. Seeing it being used with such ease was a delight. The speed at which Chinnammu and Shanguman used it to cut vegetables was fascinating, a blur of continuous motion as pieces of vegetables, cut in equal sizes, were collected in a vessel. This dexterous vertical cutting motion has been replaced by a horizontal one with knives and cutting boards in modern kitchens today.

During a recent visit to a catering company in Kochi, apart from the mechanical cutters being used for sadhya preparations, I saw a number of women using meen chattis to cut vegetables. They told me that despite all the technology that made the cooking of a sadhya more efficient, there was still some cutting that could not be done better than a meen chatti. With a machine, in order to get equally sized pieces, a lot of wastage occurs as well. It does not seem like a good idea to waste produce in order to have perfectly cut, finger-sized pieces of vegetables in dishes like avial and cubes in kaalan.

The ammi kal or grinding stone was another example of poetry in motion. The fluidity with which the two hands coordinated was always fascinating and mesmerising to watch. Chinnammu and Shanguman were kind enough to let us have a try with both the ammi kals, the flat one and the hollow one. It was a victory for us if we got the stone to slide up and down a couple of times, or turn around a few times. Did that grind the chutney or ready the batter for idlis? Obviously not. The only thing it did was make even the calm Chinnammu and Shanguman impatient, wanting to get their work done.

Today, mixer-grinders of various sizes and shapes have replaced the ammi kals. Is the chutney ground in the mixer-grinders better than that from an ammi kal? Do you get softer idlis and better dosas when you grind the batter in a mixer-grinder than an ammi kal? Is using one easier, more practical and efficient? The debate continues.

You will find many restaurants highlighting the use of ammi kals and other traditional methods to imply better-tasting food. Given my exposure to tharavad kitchens I tried to introduce some of the old methods into the modern restaurant kitchen – not an easy thing to do. The grinding section already had two large electrical stone grinders for batter and smaller ones for chutneys. These grinders use stone on stone, trying to replicate the ammi kals. I did introduce the ammi kal for chutneys but the first problem was the commis chef handling the grinding section – he had never used one. We decided to hire two elderly women who were used to the ammi kal to grind our chutneys every morning. The commis, like us as kids, would desperately try his hand at the stone, only to be frustrated.

A lot of physics is quoted – which even I have done – to talk about friction and heat when pointing towards the advantage of using an ammi kals. It was, and is, a selling point as it works. Is there a difference in the end product? Given modern technology some of the stone electrical grinders mimic the action of an ammi kal very closely. While using an ammi kal there is the option of a constant touch and feel of the end product so one knows when the required texture is reached. In the case of mixer-grinders it is a matter of stop and feel, but the end product could always be just short of the required texture and consistency, or overdone. A lot of expertise is required to know how long it will take and when to switch it off. But then, a lot of expertise is also required to handle an ammi kal. An argument in favour of modern mixer-grinders could be related to quantity. However, the old tharavad kitchens also handled large quantities to cater to hundreds of people during a sadhya.

In an Onam sadhya, especially for dishes like avial, kaalan and erissery, the ingredients used for the chutneys are similar, but the difference lies in the final texture: coarse for avial, smooth for kaalan and somewhere in between for erissery. It involves a lot of touch and feel. I use the mixer-grinder for this. The ammi kal that we have remains unused on the terrace amongst the flower pots; it is often used as a doorstopper for the terrace door. Over the years I have mastered the technique of stop-touch-feel with the mixer-grinder and have not been faulted for texture.

Large Onam sadhyas were rolled out of what were very well-designed, efficient and tightly run tharavad kitchens which procured, stored and used ingredients optimally and in a very systematic manner. Today, the sadhyas flow out of equally well-designed and efficient modern kitchens. The end products continue to be spread out on a banana leaf for a complete, balanced and tasty feast. And the sadhya remains an important event in Onam celebrations.

4

'Kaanam Vittum Onam Unnanam'

Like everything else about Onam, the sadhya today is rarely like the tharavad sadhya of yore, the one I remember from my childhood. With tharavad houses disappearing, so has large-scale home cooking. Apart from people like me who still enjoy – within the small confines of our modern kitchens – procuring the right vegetables and putting together a sadhya for family and friends, even in Kerala I found that most people today shut their kitchens for Onam and wait for the sadhya-in-a-box to be delivered! Families and friends do get together and the sadhya is served not from home kitchens but caterers. And of course, in other parts of the country, restaurants offer special sadhyas for Onam.

When I went to Kerala in my quest to uncover the Onam story, I was expecting to witness the preparation of a sadhya at a tharavad kitchen. I had reached out to many relatives and friends in Kerala to find me such a kitchen but the search yielded none. However, I did discover a similar feel at some of the catering companies I sought out. The tharavad kitchen clearly has a new home.

Sunil Thampuran is one of many caterers who, for Onam, move out from their modern kitchen to a large ground that is transformed into a kitchen. This setting took me back to the cooking areas I remember from our tharavad homes. There were ground-level fires, urulis and extra-long ladles, but everything was on an industrial scale. The activity started late at night. Scores of people were busy in innumerable kitchen activities: sorting and cleaning ingredients, cutting vegetables (some by hand, others by machines), packing completed dishes on an assembly line, at the end of which many sadhyas-in-a-box were ready for delivery. Each box was enough to serve four to six people on banana leaves, which were delivered along with the boxes. Some of the boxes were being sent abroad, as Sunil told me.

A few weeks earlier a similar operation had organised thousands of boxes with frozen, vacuum-packed sadhya containers and shipped them to various parts of the world. My brother in the UK found them at the local supermarket.

'Even if one has to sell off their property one must have an Onam sadhya.' While this old saying presumed the sadhya should be cooked at home, today it just means that for Onam you should consume a sadhya meal, be it at a restaurant or from a caterer.

As children we never felt the 'pressure' of organising an Onam sadhya. That was left to the adults to deal with. My mother unfailingly made it a point to put together a sadhya every year, especially during the times that the whole family was together.

When I left Delhi for Mumbai because of work, it was just my parents at home, so the Onam sadhya my mother cooked became a rarity. If I was lucky enough to be in Delhi at the time of the festival, I would get payasam. Once in a while I would get a little more than that, courtesy of my aunt in Mumbai. Of course, my mother would always ask, 'It's Onam, will you be home?' She would put the question to all my siblings too. It was not just a habitual refrain, I realised, but a sort of 'call' that she felt every Onam. This would strike me much later in life, especially the importance of the saying 'Kaanam vittum Onam unnanam.'[1]

It was many years later after I returned to Delhi, got married and settled down in the city that preparing a sadhya became a 'must' for me. The cooking bug had bitten, and I began enjoying kitchen duties. Hosting parties which focused on food became the norm. Since a couple of my siblings had also made Delhi their home, with a little help from them and the supervision of my mother, our Onam sadhya returned.

For the first couple of years it was only the family members who would be present. As my confidence in the kitchen grew, I became more adventurous and decided to increase the

[1] 'Even if one has to sell off their property one must have an Onam sadhya.'

number of invitees. The family itself had grown with the addition of in-laws, nieces and nephews. We also began inviting other relatives and a couple of close friends. The word spread and friends began requesting me to let them partake of the sadhya.

With requests – or rather demands – growing, and the mounting challenge to showcase my prowess in the kitchen, one fine Onam, we opened our doors for more than a dozen of our friends along with a similar number of family members. The cooking was done in a community-like fashion, my sister and sisters-in-law pitching in by cooking and bringing along a few dishes. All the house helps were put to work procuring vegetables and washing and cutting them. My mother oversaw the proceedings; she did not have a high chair like my great-grandmother, but her role was the same. Meanwhile, I was at the stove putting everything together. There was no big kitchen, no massive fires, no large urulis – just a simple four-burner gas stove, a couple of large kadais and a few large vessels. It was late-night and early-morning cooking. Our tharavad kitchen had come alive again in a new avatar!

Furniture was moved to the corners of our modest flat and space created on the floor to seat around a dozen people. We hadn't put in place any dress code, but most people turned up in Kerala sarees and mundus. For many it was a first to sit on the floor and be served a meal on banana leaves, for some it was an occasion to rekindle memories. For my family and I it was the tharavad Onam sadhya coming alive again. We served almost twenty dishes, including two payasams: palada pradhaman and nei payasam.

There was no going back! The ritual of our Onam sadhya had been established. For me, as a keen dabbler in cooking, it was the culmination of a fascination for the ritual that had been deeply ingrained in me since childhood and reinforced at the weddings of my sister and brothers. I realised that a wedding too was an occasion for a sadhya; it did not have to be just Onam. I would later extend this to other occasions like important birthdays or even just a party or an experience at a restaurant.

When my flirtations with the kitchen took on a professional turn and I became the brand chef of Zambar, a South Indian restaurant chain, my obsession with the sadhya became stronger. It moved from the modest four-burner gas stoves to large commercial stoves and brass urulis, the closest I would come to replicating a tharavad kitchen. At the first Onam hosted at Zambar, I was pleasantly surprised at the number of people that arrived for the sadhya. Many had to leave disappointed as we could not accommodate them. I realised that even in Delhi there were a large number of people who wanted to have a sadhya on Onam, and so in the years to come we extended the occasion to more than one day and across all meals. Soon, we were doing more than a thousand sadhyas for Onam, and we were not the only ones, many others were doing the same. It was not just Malayalees who came for this but a wide spectrum of people. For Malayalees, it was the convenience of not having to cook the same food at home that was the draw.

The feast on a leaf has become popular across the country and in many parts of the world. But there is more to the Onam sadhya than that – it reflects a way of life that is in consonance with nature and fits in with today's concerns of well-being.

Sadhya.
TRADITIONAL KERALA SADHYA
HARITHAMPANS
CURR WORLD
POORNASREE CATERING
രാജനഗരിയുടെ രുചി രാജ്യമെങ്ങും
www.curryworld.in
KERALA'S FIRST TRADITIONAL SADHYA CURRIES OUTLET
TRIPUNITHURA +91 79947 11601
RAVIPURAM +91 97456 11601
EDAPPALLY +91 95670 11601
KAKKANAD +91 98461 11601
A NEW VENTURE OF K HARI THAMPAN SONS

5

Farm to Leaf

Both our tharavads were surrounded by paddy fields, vegetable patches, fruit orchards, cowsheds and a large pond. For us children it was a very large playground, many times the size of a football field. It was left to our imagination as to what we could do in it.

Apart from the usual aimless running around and trying to pluck fruit, off trees, one type of activity that remains vivid in my mind is our interactions with the right-hand men of the tharavads, Shanguman and Raman Nair. While Shanguman was a man who wore many hats and became a 'child' when with us, Raman was a sombre, no-nonsense person who went about his daily tasks with a serious air. It is him I remember trying to teach us about vegetables and fruits.

Today, some of the catchphrases in the restaurant world are 'farm to table', 'farm to fork' and 'seasonal'. When I think about those days with Raman and Shanguman I realise that we are reintroducing lost practices.

At the tharavads, we ate what was available and grown in the fields and orchards around us with the produce depending on the season. Unlike in the city, we were more than happy to wake up at the crack of dawn. Being in sunlit areas was a welcome escape for us after the darkness with imaginary shadows and noises that enveloped the tharavads post sunset. Sometimes, at sunrise, we would accompany Raman to the cowshed to milk the cows. That activity was great fun, unlike the moment we actually had to drink the milk at breakfast.

On lucky days we would go with Raman for an even bigger task: plucking coconuts or jackfruit. Raman would literally sprint up a coconut tree and chop off a bunch of coconuts with a knife. He would then sort them through a shaking and knocking process, chopping up a couple so we could drink the water in them. Then he would slit them and make a scoop using a piece of the outer shell with which we were able to scrape the kernel and eat it!

Chinnammu, after a bath in the pond and offering prayers to the deity installed at the tharavad, would get busy in the kitchen. Raman would pick up a few coconuts from the store room, and split and break them. We would eagerly wait with tumblers in our hands to collect the water and drink it. Chinnammu would then get down to grating the coconuts with a meen chatti that served the dual purpose of grating coconuts and cutting vegetables. We would sit around her, eyes on the plate that was collecting the grated coconut, waiting for the odd piece that would break off, un-grated, which we would grab and eat.

She would then move to the ammi kal, the flat grating stone, with the coconut. Just outside the kitchen was a small green patch from where she would pluck some chillies, coriander and curry leaves off the plants. She would sit down, legs astride the flat stone, and place the grated coconut, green chillies and coriander leaves on it, sprinkling some water as well. Then, with the cylindrical stone she would first smash the coconut in a seesaw motion, sprinkle some more water and then in a continuous motion run the cylindrical stone up and down the flat stone. The mesmerising movement slowly yielded a chutney ready to be garnished with a tempering of mustard, red chilli and curry leaves. She would put some of the grated coconut into water (to squeeze milk out later) and keep a little aside for garnishing.

After breakfast, depending on the weather and the season, if it was not raining or too sunny, we would tag along with Raman to the vegetable patch. It had pumpkins and gourds all over, growing wild, almost. Various creepers and plants with beans, okra and brinjal.

Tapioca and yam peeping out of the ground. We would carry a couple of bamboo baskets and wait on the fringes of the vegetable patch, wary of stepping in and finding darting reptiles. We would pluck beans from creepers close to us and eat them raw. Raman would go around knocking at the gourds, lightly pinching beans and clearing the top soil to check on yams and tapioca. This process allowed him to determine what was ready to be plucked. A pumpkin perhaps, or some gourd, yam or tapioca. Some beans and okra if they were ready. All this would be put into baskets and we would take them to the house to be sorted by Chinnammu and my grandmother. What had to be cooked was decided and lunch preparations would start.

In the days prior to Onam, Vishu or any other celebration there would be a Jackfruit Day. Of course, our visits were occasion enough to have a Jackfruit Day. This was the day ripe jackfruit was brought for a couple of preparations: jackfruit chips, plain and sweet, and chakkavarathi. Plus, we got to eat the fruit and have a delicious payasam made from it. Not to mention the stir-fry made from the seeds.

Jackfruit-hunting ended up being a day-long activity which involved a lot of scouting by Raman. We would go from tree to tree, checking for ripe fruit that was easily accessible. The trees were very tall and not easy to climb. The ground below would have overripe jackfruit, fallen and split open, a rotten, sweet smell filling the air. Once a tree with the largest number of ripe fruits was identified we would head back to a little shed next to the cattle. This was filled with various field implements: yokes, harvesting tools, rope and large bamboo poles.

Raman would choose a long, sturdy pole. To the end of this he would tie a sickle, which he would sharpen on a granite stone. His assistants would join and help him. They would carry what looked like a fishing net, and we would all go back to the chosen tree. The net would be opened and spread out below, the corners tied to trees nearby like a trampoline sheet a few feet above the ground. With deft hands, skill and strength, Raman would saw at the stems of the ripe fruit while all of us waited, staring in anticipation. Amid rustling leaves, the fruit would fall into the net.

These fruits were truly large, some of them a couple of feet tall so we children couldn't even encompass them fully with our arms. Raman and his assistants would carry them back to the house. We followed, cheering as if returning from a successful hunt.

The fruits would be placed in the verandah outside the kitchen. Chinnammu had placed some oil for all of us to rub on our palms. The fruit was cut into small quarters, with each of us getting one. The quarter would be bent so that the fleshy petals or pods were jutting out and the strings or rind holding them broke. The oil prevented the white juice from the outer layers of the fruit from sticking to our fingers.

The pods were plucked out and then split to remove the seed. While we managed to pry one pod, the help would have finished a whole quarter. We would of course be eating most of the pods that we removed.

A couple of women who worked in the paddy fields would clean out the fruit and cut them for chips. Some would be kept aside for the payasam to be made and some for the chakkavarathi. The outer skin would be bundled off to the cattle shed. It would be a treat of the day for the cattle too. We would, if we were lucky, get to feed them the jackfruit remains.

Meanwhile, Raman and Chinnammu would handle the cooking, for which large urulis and iron kadais had been taken out from the store room cleaned and kept ready. While the cooking got underway, the children were shooed away from the kitchen as there was a lot of hot oil and the kitchen would be steaming. We would pick up a handful of the jackfruit seeds and rush off to the courtyard to play inventive games with them. At the end of the day there would be nothing of the jackfruit remaining; all of it would have been put to use.

Like the Jackfruit Day, there would be a Banana Day too. From the banana orchard, fully grown bunches or hands of bananas (the Kerala variety, nendran pazham or etha kaaya) were cut. Some were tied with a rope and hung from the roof to ripen. Others were used for making chips. The rest of the plant was cut at the root, and the leaves, not torn, were sent to the kitchen and used not just to eat off but for various preparations that called for leaf coverings. The stem was split open and the inner white kernel was also used to make a stir-fried thoran. The leftovers went to the cowshed.

Looking back, now one realises the self-sufficiency that existed in these tharavads. We did not value it much then, and we yearn for it now. When it came to an Onam sadhya too the preparations revolved around what was available within the tharavad. At varying intervals, days before or on the sadhya day, ingredients were procured and processed for use immediately or on a later day. The tharavad sadhya ticked all the boxes of today's concerns of going local, minimal wastage and maintaining the balance of nature, some of which continue in the preparation of the modern Onam sadhya.

A traditional Onam sadhya was prepared using locally sourced and seasonal ingredients grown in the vicinity of the household.

Many of the vegetables, fruits and spices used were harvested from the family's garden or orchard, or purchased from a local market. This ensured that the ingredients were fresh and at their peak of flavour, reducing the need for long-distance transportation. Today, of course, one relies on better preservation and packaging techniques and faster transportation to get the freshest produce possible.

The sadhya dishes were and still are prepared with minimal processing, emphasising the use of whole, unprocessed ingredients. For example, fresh vegetables are used in their natural state and spices are typically ground or used in their whole form. This minimal processing preserves the flavours and nutritional value of the ingredients.

The sadhya menu was influenced by the seasonal availability of ingredients, with the celebrations taking place during the harvest season of Chingam in Kerala. The use of seasonal produce not only ensured freshness but also supported local agriculture and reduced the need for storing food for extended periods. Today, we do try to use the same ingredients though substitutes have begun creeping in.

In many cases, the individuals or families preparing the traditional sadhya were directly involved in cultivating the ingredients in their garden or fields. This direct connection to the source promoted sustainability, reduced the carbon footprint associated with transportation, and supported local farmers and agriculture.

The sadhya is a communal feast often prepared by multiple family members, with each person contributing specific dishes. This sense of community involvement and tradition strengthens local and familial bonds as it brings people together to celebrate the harvest and the abundance of the land.

Sadhya dishes typically involve using all parts of an ingredient. For example, various parts of the coconut tree – from the coconut fruit to coconut water, coconut milk and coconut oil – are used in different dishes. This approach minimises food wastage, aligning with the principles of sustainability. It is an excellent example of the farm-to-leaf concept as it epitomises the use of locally sourced seasonal ingredients, minimal processing, direct connections to the source and sustainability.

6

Left to Right

Serving an Onam sadhya is quite a challenge, and one which goes beyond simply cooking the twenty-four-plus dishes. If it is a family sadhya, confusion and chaos sets in from the moment you begin placing the leaves on which the meal will be served.

Should the narrow tail end of the leaf be on the left or right? There is some disagreement about this. The tail end should be on the left of the person who is eating. Sometimes you do not get leaves which have a tail and a head, they are almost rectangular pieces because they have been trimmed to remove the torn portions. In this case the leaf could be placed without bothering about left and right. This was just one of the problems I faced when I managed the first Onam sadhya at the restaurant I was heading.

The left-and-right business seems simple to understand, but there is a lot of confusion when you are in the centre trying to explain it to the serving staff. While I was doing my best to demonstrate the left and right side of the leaves from the point of view of the person being served, my restaurant manager decided to make it even simpler: he told them to place the leaf with the tail to their own right.

We started a mock drill. It led to the leaves being laid out all wrong. The manager was adding to the mayhem by screaming, 'Tumhara left kaunsa hai ... is side se right ... nahin, is side se right.'

I put a stop to the whole exercise. Back to square one. The instruction was simple. Place the leaf with the tail to the left of the person eating. It worked after a few tries. I could see some service staff standing at the table, twisting their heads to see which way the person would be seated, then placing the leaf correctly.

The manager, of course, wanting to have the last word, suggested that we cut off the tail and use rectangular pieces of the leaves; that way there would be no confusion. He would understand later that it was simpler to use the whole leaf as service would become easier. Using a full leaf, with a narrow tail end and a broad head end, fits into the serving scheme of a sadhya. And what is that?

The more people you talk to, the more variations you get. And if you begin checking online you may have to postpone your sadhya for a year as you wallow in a sea of confusion, and endless permutations and combinations.

Meanwhile, at the front of the house in the restaurant, as the leaves kept going left and right there was another problem brewing at the back of the house, in the kitchen. Many of the chefs were from Tamil Nadu and they had their own versions for the preparation of dishes, especially the sambar, avial, kootu and thorans. This is not the place to get into the debate of who was right.

To me, it was clear. It was Onam. We were to serve a traditional Nair sadhya, influenced by what was served at my tharavad home. So, days before the meal, through many trials, much to the disapproving looks of the chefs, I had to modify the recipes so we could come as close as possible to the sadhya I had in mind.

The avial became a bone of contention. My head chef wanted to play with colours – rightly so, to an extent – and wished to introduce vegetables like carrots to add a touch of orange to the otherwise yellowish curry with green highlights. This led to me lecturing him about how carrot was not a vegetable native to Kerala, and the concept of an avial with four seasonal vegetables: two types of pumpkin – yellow and white – raw banana and string beans. If required, one of the vegetables, preferably the string beans, could be replaced by yam. Over the years, after a lot of appreciation from clients, the chefs got happier about following my Nair recipes.

Back to the front of the house. The service staff and the leaves had settled into the right orientation, but the serving of items was a more daunting task. The trays, which the service staff normally used with utmost ease, were replaced with chomukhas serving vessels with four containers. The staff's trousers were replaced by mundus (the sarong-like garment worn in many parts of South India). They were very excited, but when they tried walking they looked like geishas in kimonos, taking short, shuffling steps, gingerly and slowly, afraid the mundu would come off.

Every day, for about a week leading up to the Onam sadhya, the manager's normal morning and evening briefing was extended by thirty minutes as he put the service staff through their paces in mundus. He would make them walk up and down the length of the restaurant, getting them to slowly be more comfortable and easier with their strides.

Then came the order of serving the various items and their placement on the leaves. That added more time to the briefing. At first, on a blackboard, I drew out the leaf and explained where each item had to be served. The manager repeated this exercise daily, turning it into a quiz by getting the staff members to mark the placements on a leaf drawn on the blackboard. I pitied them at one level. It was not only the right placement they had to memorise, but also the names of the dishes. The restaurant menu, in its Kerala vegetarian section, only had a few sadhya items like avial, thoran, erissery and pachadi.

A few days before the big day, the kitchen did a couple of full trials and we had the staff carry out service on a mock table. The manager had distributed chomukhas to a few, some were given responsibility to handle the accompaniments, some the rasam, buttermilk and payasams that were to be served in glasses and bowls. A hesitant start slowly but surely moved on to a fairly smooth execution. They took their time and referred to the blackboard when in doubt. But the mock trial was deceptive.

On Onam it started with the manager and me going around tables correcting the placement of some leaves. By and large it was fine. Before people walked in, we supervised the placement of the accompaniments. That was also fine. Then, the storm hit. Customers began walking in simultaneously, and as it happens, every table was in that much more of a hurry than the next. They all wanted to be served first.

The parade of the service staff with chomukhas began. They were calm and poised, delicately serving the items in the sequence that had been drilled into them. As the restaurant became full, demands and pressures from customers increased, and panic and chaos struck. The man serving the parippu and ghee, following the one serving the rice, lost his way, while the ones with the thorans and mains were trying to set speed records. The smooth flow of the assembly line was disturbed. The man with the bucket of sambar decided to strike even before diners had finished with the parippu and ghee.

It took just that small slip to send the entire service into a spin and it was not long before the kitchen felt its effects.

Some customers got double helpings and some missed out on a few dishes as the rushing service staff clashed with each other and the chefs in the kitchen. Payasam was poured over rice. Sambar was served in bowls. The process of refilling the chomukhas inside the kitchen led to a total mix-up. Avial was put into the erissery container, kootu curry in the avial one, the thorans were mixed up and the pal payasam took on a brownish tinge as it was poured into the pradhaman container. The sadhya took on the hues of a fusion meal.

The manager and I were firefighting, trying to bring some order into the assembly line, cool tempers in the kitchen and reorganise the chomukhas. We were also rushing from table to table, apologising and trying to correct mix-ups. But my first sadhya at the restaurant was not as much of a nightmare as we thought it was. Surprisingly, the customers gave us the benefit of the doubt, and left with smiles and promises to return the following year.

It is not easy serving a sadhya for sixty to eighty people. A lot of training and practise is required to achieve the fluidity and ease one sees in sadhyas for hundreds at Onam in Kerala. By the next Onam my staff managed to be, if not perfect, very fluent in both preparation and service, so much so that on one particular Onam – my last with the restaurant – we served a record number of a thousand-plus sadhyas! The sadhyas at home were easier as I had the help of my mother and other family members. It was the practice that I got there which I carried to the restaurant and my other catering gigs.

There is science and a little bit of ayurveda involved. A sadhya is a balance of six tastes: sweet, sour, salty, bitter, pungent and astringent. They are all present, some singularly and others in a mix. A sadhya is also a melody of textures, from crisp to soft to watery. Here, putting together the science, ayurveda, textures and my observations from what I have seen and been told by the elders in the family, is a largely acceptable way to serve the Onam sadhya:

Prior to inviting people to sit for the meal, place the leaves with the tail to the left of the person eating. The left corner is for all the accompaniments: a pinch of salt, pickles, chips, a banana, ela ada/unniyappam and pappadum. Towards the right upper half put some pulli inji and inji thayir. Put a tablespoon full of payasam in the lower, right-hand corner.

Now, between these two ends, running clockwise, comes the rest. After everyone is seated, begin with the thorans, serving them in the upper part of the leaf, starting from where the chips are placed. Below this put drier preparations like avial, erissery, kootu kari and kaalan. On the right-hand side serve the runny preparations like theeyal, olan and pulissery. Leave the lower centre half for the rice.

After the rice is served, pour a few teaspoons of parippu followed by ghee. The meal begins with that. Then comes the sambar. And the sadhya is on.

On the periphery of the leaf, either above the centre or on the right, you could place buttermilk and rasam in tumblers or glasses. The payasam could also be placed in bowls next to them. For the truly deft diners all this is served on the leaf.

What you have on the leaf is an array of tastes, flavours and textures, from the salty and pungent left side to sweet and sour at the other end, with bitter and astringent in between.

In fact, when you look at the narrow left corner, you would find it packed with all the tastes: salty (salt, pickles), sweet (banana–jaggery chips, ela ada, unniyappam), pungent and bitter (pickles), sour and astringent (pulli inji and inji thayir).

In terms of texture, you have the crisp pappadums and chips on the left, the firm but soft curries in the middle and the watery olan, pulissery and theeyal to the right. With all this left corner, right corner, centre and the centre half, it sounds like a football match!

Now everything is served. But how does one eat a sadhya? Definitely with your hands, but in what order? Traditionally, as soon as you sit down to eat, the accompaniments would already be on the leaf. Eat the chips, taste the pulli inji and inji thayir. Purists would check the payasam, a teaspoon of which would be placed along with the accompaniments. There is a little controversy regarding the first course, which is the parippu with ghee. Crush a little pappadum into this. These days the parippu is followed by sambar, but according to my aunt, Radha Thampuran, after parippu you had the erissery, kaalan, avial, olan, pachadi and pulissery along with the thorans. The last two courses before the payasams, according to her, were sambar followed by rasam. And after the payasams you had some rice with the sambaram or buttermilk. Anything more on the leaf was eaten between these dishes.

These days, few people venture to have rasam or sambaram with rice as it is not an easy task to handle these flowing liquids on the leaf. Remember to start with small quantities of rice. It is served continuously, as are the other items when required. There is a way to indicate you do not want to be served more, by extending your hand, palms down, over the leaf. I have tried employing this constantly, especially with liquid curries like olan, but I have been reprimanded by the person serving, asking me to remove my hand. The first serving of the dish cannot be avoided. My idea was to have the chips on the left of the leaf, a little bit of rice served in the middle with parippu and sambar and get to the payasams.

When the curries were served at home, I would see my elders dipping a finger into them as they were served and tasting them. Follow the elders and do as they do. It was exactly what we kids did when it came to consuming a sadhya. Step by step we followed their cues. If they took a bit of avial, we did the same. If they reached out to the olan, we did too. Purists would argue about the order of not just the serving of the sadhya but the order in which it is to be eaten: should the avial come first or the erissery, should the theeyal be served or placed on the leaf; what about the pulissery? There is no end to the debate. Enjoy it the way you feel.

A Feast for Many Occasions

You don't have to wait for Onam. Any celebration is excuse enough to serve a sadhya, be it a wedding, birthday, special occasion or just a party! Given that you have more than twenty dishes to play around with, there are many permutations and combinations possible in case you don't want to serve a full Onam sadhya, yet would like to keep the essential feel of one. For an intimate twosome to a family of six, or a party of eight or ten, the sadhya can be curated accordingly.

The following menu possibilities provide a range of options, from a simple and quick meal to a more comprehensive and balanced sadhya. You can mix and match based on your preferences and the number of dishes you'd like to prepare. With a few tweaks, it can also be suitable for those who follow a vegan or gluten-free diet.

THE FULL SADHYA

Here is an extensive list of various dishes that could be included in a sadhya. The usual Onam sadhya would include over twenty dishes, so you can pick and choose.

Menu

Accompaniments

Kaaya Varuthatha (Banana Chips)

Chakka Chola Varuthatha (Jackfruit Chips)

Sarkara Upperi (Jaggery-coated Banana Chips)

Chenna Varuthatha (Yam Fry)

Naranga Achar (Lime Pickle)

Manga Kari (Mango Pickle)

Pulli Inji (Tamarind–Ginger Pickle)

Inji Thayir (Ginger–Curd Relish)

Sambaram (Buttermilk)

Pappadum

Thorans and Upperis

Beetroot Thoran (Beetroot Stir-fry)

Muttakose Thoran (Cabbage Stir-fry)

Achinga/Payaru Thoran

(String Beans Stir-fry)

Padavalanga Thoran (Snake Gourd Stir-fry)

Kaaya Upperi (Raw Banana Stir-fry)

Cheera Thoran (Red Spinach Stir-fry)

Staple

Matta Ari (Kerala Brown Rice)

Mains

Parippu (Lentil Curry)

Avial (Vegetables in Coconut Chutney)

Erissery (Pumpkin Curry)

Kaalan (Yam and Raw Banana Curry)

Olan (Pumpkin Stew)

Kootu Kari (Mixed Vegetable Curry)

Pulissery (Curd Curry)

Ulli Theeyal (Shallot Curry)

Sambar (Vegetables and Lentil Curry)

Rasam (Lentil Soup)

Desserts

Palada Payasam (Rice Flakes and Milk Dessert)

Ada/Chakka/Pazham Pradhaman (Rice Flakes/Jackfruit/Banana, Jaggery and Coconut Milk Dessert)

Parippu Payasam (Lentil Dessert)

Pal Payasam (Rice and Milk Dessert)

Nei Payasam (Rice and Jaggery Pudding)

Unniyappam (Sweet Rice Flour Dumplings)

Ela Ada (Steamed Pancakes)

Pazham Pori (Banana Fritters)

Steamed Bananas

SADHYA FOR TWO

Creating a sadhya for an intimate twosome can be a special and memorable experience. For an authentic touch, serve the meal on banana leaves, which are not just biodegradable but add to the traditional experience. Create a romantic ambience with candlelight and soft music to make the intimate occasion even more special. Consider wearing traditional Kerala attire, such as a mundu and kasavu saree. Decorate your dining area with fresh jasmine or marigold flowers.

Menu

Sambaram

Pulli Inji

Pappadum

Pickle (Mango or Lime)

Avial

Thoran (Choose any one as per available vegetables)

Kerala Rice

Parippu and Ghee

Sambar

Pal Payasam

Serving Tips

Begin with a refreshing glass of sambaram, the spiced buttermilk drink, served in a glass, to whet your appetite. Place the banana leaf with the narrow end to the left of the person eating. Place the pappadum and a pinch of salt on the lower left end of the leaf. Just above this put some pickle and pulli inji. On the upper centre half serve some avial and thoran, and below it the rice. Start your meal with a tablespoon of parippu and a teaspoon of ghee poured over the rice. Follow the parippu with sambar. The avial can be had separately with rice. The thoran can be had with both the sambar and the avial. Dip into the pickle and pulli inji with your fingertips for a burst of new flavours. The pappadum, in bits and pieces, will add a crunchy touch to the meal. Conclude your sadhya with payasam, served in a bowl.

DAILY SADHYA

A variation of sadhya can be had by a family of three or four members as a special meal for lunch on a Sunday or on a holiday. To create some excitement and break the monotony of daily meals try and dress up, preferably in mundus and kasavus. If you can sit on the floor, do that, or else the table is fine. Use banana leaves, again to break the monotony of using regular plates. You can avoid a repetition of the same menu by replacing certain dishes.

Here are two possible menus.

Menu 1

Kaaya Varuthatha

Sambaram

Pulli Inji

Pappadum

Pickle (Mango or Lime)

Avial

Erissery

Pulissery

Thoran (Choose any one as per available vegetables)

Menu 2

Chenna Varuthatha

Rasam

Pulli Inji

Pappadum

Pickle (Mango or Lime)

Kootu Kari

Olan

Kaalan

Thoran (Choose any one as per available vegetables)

Kerala Rice

Parippu

Ulli Theeyal

Ada Pradhaman

Serving Tips

Place the banana leaf with the narrow end to the left of the person eating. Pour a glass of sambaram or rasam, to be had as a refreshing drink, palate cleanser or meal finisher. Place the pappadum and a pinch of salt on the lower left end of the leaf. Just above this put some pickle, pulli inji and kaya varuthatha or chenna varuthatha. On the upper half of the leaf serve some avial or kootu curry, erissery or olan, pulissery or kaalan and thoran. Below this, in the middle, serve the rice. Start your meal with a tablespoon of parippu and a teaspoon of ghee poured over the rice. Follow the parippu with sambar or ulli theeyal. The curries can be had separately with rice. The thoran can be had with both the sambar/theeyal and curries. Conclude the sadhya with pal payasam or ada pradhaman, served in bowls.

SADHYA-THEMED PARTY

What do you do when you don't have the space, don't want to use banana leaves, want to serve drinks and snacks before the main meal but still want it to be a sadhya? Have a sadhya-themed party! Ask guests to come in traditional Kerala attire. Use jasmine and marigold flowers to decorate the house.

For a gathering with more than eight to ten people it is not always possible to serve a sadhya in the traditional way, on banana leaves. Of course, if you have the space there's nothing like replicating the authentic way of serving: on banana leaves, on the floor or a long table set indoors or outdoors. The following instructions tell you how to serve a regular Onam sadhya with two possible menus.

Menu 1

Drinks

Apart from the drinks you want to serve at your party, do try these two options.

Sambaram: Serve cold as a non-alcoholic drink

Rasam Cocktail: Add a white spirit, like vodka or gin, to rasam that has been sieved, and serve cold.

Snacks

Kaaya Varuthatha

Chakka Chola Varuthatha

Chenna Varuthatha

Kaaya Upperi

Mains

Pickle (Lime or Mango)

Pulli Inji

Inji Thayir

Ghee

Parippu

Sambar

Avial

Erissery

Pulissery

Thoran (Choose any two as per available vegetables)

Rice

Pappadum

Desserts

Choose any two payasams, preferably one white (pal payasam, palada payasam) and one dark (ada pradhaman, parippu payasam, chakka or banana pradhaman).

Menu 2

Drinks

Apart from the drinks you want to serve at your party, do try these two options.

Sambaram: Serve cold as a non-alcoholic option

Rasam Cocktail: Add a white spirit, like vodka or gin, to rasam that has been sieved, and serve cold.

Snacks

Kaaya Varuthatha

Chakka Chola Varuthatha

Chenna Varuthatha

Kaaya Upperi

Mains

Pickle (Mango or Lime)

Pulli Inji

Inji Thayir

Ghee

Parippu

Ulli Theeyal

Kootu Curry

Olan

Kaalan

Thoran (Choose any two as per available vegetables)

Rice

Pappadum

Desserts

Choose any two payasams, preferably one white (pal payasam, palada payasam) and one dark (ada pradhaman, parippu payasam, chakka or banana pradhaman)

Serving Tips

Treat this as a buffet. The drinks can be served at a counter and the snacks placed in platters on tables or passed around. The mains can be served in bowls – small ones for the accompaniments and large ones for the curries and thorans. The rice can be on a platter and the pappadum in a bread basket. The payasams can be served in dessert bowls.

You may increase the number of dishes to make it more elaborate.

VEGAN SADHYA

While the traditional Onam sadhya is vegetarian, with a few tweaks it is possible to make it a vegan one too. Curd is used in some dishes like kaalan and cucumber pulissery, and milk in dishes like palada payasam and pal payasam. Ghee is added to parippu, or is used in roasting cashew nuts and raisins for the payasams. If these dishes are excluded you still have an extensive menu from which you can pick and choose.

Menu

Accompaniments

Kaaya Varuthatha

Chenna Varuthatha

Sarkara Upperi

Manga Kari

Naranga Achar

Pulli Inji

Pappadum

Thorans and Upperis

Beetroot Thoran

Muttakose Thoran

Achinga or Payaru Thoran

Padavalanga Thoran

Kaaya Upperi

Cheera Thoran

Mains

Avial

Erissery

Olan

Kootu Curry

Sambar

Ulli Theeyal

Rasam

Desserts

Moong Dal Payasam

Ada Pradhaman

Chakka or Banana Pradhaman

Unniyappam

Pazham Pori

Steamed Bananas

If you want have vegan versions of dishes like kaalan, puliserry and payasam, use substitutes (see Appendix 1). Remember, the use of soya, almond or other plant-based milks would to an extent add their own flavour, as would curd made from these dairy substitutes. The feel and texture would by and large be the same. For the payasams do not use ghee to roast the nuts and raisins; use regular refined oil.

GLUTEN-FREE SADHYA

Today, the number of people seeking gluten-free food is on the rise. There are people who are allergic to wheat-based products and others for whom it is a lifestyle choice. The Onam sadhya in its traditional form is entirely gluten-free. It is perhaps one of the few such elaborate meals that is so.

One has to be careful when using lentils to make sure there is no cross-contamination involved. While the recommended coconut oil is gluten-free, if you are using a substitute please ensure it does not contain any gluten product.

The only dessert that contains gluten is pazham pori, which uses maida. It is not an essential dish in an Onam sadhya and you could easily exclude it without affecting the experience. If you would like to include it use a recommended substitute (see Appendix 1) for maida.

Let us look at the dishes in a sadhya that can be served in a gluten-free menu.

Menu

Accompaniments

Kaaya Varuthatha

Sarkara Upperi

Chenna Varuthatha

Manga Kari

Naranga Achar

Pulli Inji

Inji Thayir

Mains

Parippu (lentils and ghee)

Avial (vegetables, coconut, curd, green chillies, spices and condiments)

Erissery (pumpkin, red lobia, coconut, spices and condiments)

Kaalan (vegetables, coconut, curd, spices and condiments)

Olan (vegetables, coconut milk, spices and condiments)

Kootu Kari (vegetables, chickpeas, spices and condiments)

Vellarikai Pulissery (cucumber, coconut, curd, spices and condiments)

Ulli Theeyal (onions, coconut, tamarind, coconut, spices and condiments)

Sambar (vegetables, lentils, tamarind, spices and condiments)

Rasam (lentils, tamarind, spices and condiments)

Thorans and Upperis

Muttakose Thoran (cabbage, spices and condiments)

Beetroot Thoran (beetroot, spices and condiments)

Kaaya Upperi (raw banana, spices and condiments)

Padavalanga Thoran (snake gourd, spices and condiments)

Achinga/Payaru Thoran (string beans, spices and condiments)

Cheera Thoran (red spinach, spices and condiments)

Payasams

Palada payasam (rice flakes, milk, sugar, ghee, cardamom, cashew nuts and raisins)

Ada Pradhaman (rice flakes, jaggery, coconut milk, ghee, cardamom, cashew nuts and raisins)

Parippu Payasam (lentils, jaggery, coconut milk, ghee, cardamom, cashew nuts and raisins)

Chakka Pradhaman (jackfruit, jaggery, coconut milk, ghee, cardamom, cashew nuts and raisins)

Banana Pradhaman (bananas, jaggery, coconut milk, ghee, cardamom, cashew nuts and raisins)

Pal Payasam (rice, milk, sugar, ghee, cardamom, cashew nuts and raisins)

Nei Payasam (rice, jaggery, ghee, cardamom, cashew nuts and raisins)

Other Sadhya Desserts

Unniyappam (rice, lentils, bananas, jaggery, coconut and cardamom)

Ela Ada (rice/rice flour, jaggery, coconut and cardamom)

Steamed Bananas

VEGAN, GLUTEN-FREE SADHYA

It has become necessary today when you invite people over for a meal that you check their dietary restrictions. Increasingly, you will find the words 'vegan' and 'gluten-free' being mentioned. We have seen how a sadhya can be easily adapted for people who prefer vegan or gluten-free meals without robbing it of its unique spread. It is not uncommon to have people who prefer both vegan and gluten-free meals. The feast on a leaf can still be had while accommodating these two dietary restrictions together.

Menu

Accompaniments

Kaaya Varuthatha

Chenna Varuthatha

Sarkara Upperi

Manga Kari

Naranga Achar

Pulli Inji

Pappadum

Mains

Parippu Curry (do not serve ghee with it)

Avial

Erissery

Olan

Kootu Kari

Sambar

Ulli Theeyal

Rasam

Thorans and Upperis

Beetroot Thoran

Muttakose Thoran

Achinga/Payaru Thoran

Padavalanga Thoran

Kaaya Upperi

Cheera Thoran

Desserts

Moong Dal Payasam

Ada Pradhaman

Chakka/Banana Pradhaman

Unniyappam

RECIPES

ACCOMPANIMENTS

In an Onam sadhya the tail end of the banana leaf, on your left, is loaded with accompaniments that range from sweet and salty to sour and pungent. You will find the six ayurvedic tastes here, as well as a spectrum of textures: from crisp to soft and liquid.

These accompaniments are placed on the leaf prior to the actual service of the sadhya. As children we were allowed to do some of these placements, especially the banana and chips.

Grown-ups would tell us to place around four or five chips on each leaf. We would count them out precisely, making sure that there was not one less or one more. Needless to say, after putting some on every leaf a couple of chips would go into our mouths. Since I have a sweet tooth, I would always prefer to distribute the *sarkara upperi*, the jaggery-coated banana chips.

There is no fixed number of accompaniments that can be served at an Onam sadhya. The poovan pazham (small variety of ripe banana), kaaya varuthatha, sarkara upperi, manga kari or naranga achar, pulli inji/inji thayir and pappadum are usually a must. To this you could add chakka chola varuthatha, a second pickle, steamed Kerala banana, ela ada or unniyappam.

Very few people today actually make the chips and pickles at home. These are readily available at South Indian stores or online. If you are unable to find the poovan pazham, you could substitute it with the regular robusta bananas. Pulli inji is also available in bottles today, though making it is fairly simple.

Kaaya Varuthatha

Banana Chips

A traditional Kerala snack and an integral part of sadhyas, these are made with the nendran or etha kaaya variety of bananas, often called the Kerala banana.

Prep Time	**Cook Time**	**Serves**
15–20 minutes	20–25 minutes	15–20

Ingredients

4–5 green, mature but not ripe Kerala bananas

½ teaspoon + ½ teaspoon turmeric powder

Oil to fry (preferably coconut oil)

Salt to taste

Nutritional Value

(Per serving of 25 g)

Calories: 50–160 kcal

Fat: 9–10 g

Carbohydrates: 17–20 g

Fibre: 2–3 g

Sugar: <1 g

Protein: 1–2 g

Sodium: Varies but is generally low, typically less than 10 mg

Instructions

1. Peel the bananas and keep them in a bowl of water mixed with ½ teaspoon turmeric powder for 10–15 minutes. This helps to maintain the colour and prevents the bananas from turning brown.
2. Pat the bananas dry. Slice them as thinly as possible, so they are almost translucent, with the help of a slicer/mandolin. Drop them in a bowl of water so that they do not get discoloured. You could also use a knife depending on your cutting skills.
3. Dissolve ½ teaspoon turmeric and salt in a cup of water. Keep aside.
4. Heat oil in a deep, heavy-bottomed pan or kadai over medium heat. The oil should be hot but not smoking.
5. Pat dry a batch of banana slices with the help of a kitchen towel. Gently slide them into the hot oil, making sure not to overcrowd the pan. Add a couple of teaspoons of the turmeric–salt water. (This not only adds salt to the chips but also gives them a yellow colour.) Be careful, the oil will splutter. Fry them until they turn crisp and golden-brown. This may take a few minutes per batch.

   It is preferable, if using a slicer, to slice the bananas – after soaking in turmeric water and patting them dry with a kitchen towel – directly into the oil.
6. Remove the fried banana chips using a slotted spoon and drain them on paper towels to remove excess oil.
7. Repeat the process for all the sliced bananas
8. Allow the banana chips to cool completely before storing them in an airtight container. They will stay fresh for several weeks.

The banana peels can be used to make a simple stir-fried thoran. Lightly scrape them and chop finely. Follow the string beans thoran recipe.

Chakka Chola Varuthatha

Jackfruit Chips

Ripe jackfruit chips, also known as chakka chola varuthatha in Malayalam, are a delightful snack enjoyed in Kerala and other parts of South India. It is served as one of the accompaniments during a sadhya.

Prep Time

30–45 minutes

Cook Time

20–30 minutes

Serves

15–20

Ingredients

1 medium-sized ripe jackfruit (5–8 kg) or 450 g jackfruit pods

250 ml oil for deep frying

Salt to taste (optional)

Nutritional Value

(Per serving of 25 g)

Calories: 50–160 kcal

Fat: 8–10 g

Carbohydrates: 20–25 g

Fibre: 1–2 g

Sugar: 10–15 g

Protein: <1 g

Sodium: If salt is used, it is less than 10 mg

Instructions

1. Start by selecting a ripe jackfruit. You'll want to choose one that is fully ripe, fragrant and sweet.
2. Cut and peel the jackfruit to remove the ripe pods.
3. Cut the pods, remove the seeds and the white pith surrounding them.
4. Slice the pods into long, thin slices. You can use a knife or sharp kitchen scissors for this. Try to make the slices as uniform as possible to ensure even frying.
5. Heat oil for deep frying in a deep pan or kadai over medium heat.
6. Once the oil is hot, carefully add the jackfruit slices in batches, making sure not to overcrowd the pan. Fry in batches to ensure even cooking.
7. Fry the jackfruit slices until they turn golden-brown and crisp. This usually takes 5–7 minutes per batch.
8. Using a slotted spoon, remove the fried jackfruit chips from the oil and place them on a plate lined with paper towels to drain excess oil.
9. If desired, sprinkle salt over the hot chips for added flavor. Be careful not to oversalt, as ripe jackfruit is naturally sweet.
10. Repeat the frying process with the remaining jackfruit slices until all are fried.
11. Once all the jackfruit chips are fried and drained, allow them to cool completely before serving.
12. The chips can be stored in an airtight container once they have cooled completely to maintain their crispness.

Sarkara Upperi

Jaggery-Coated Banana Chips

Sweet chips made with the nendran/etha kaaya variety of bananas which are coated in jaggery. A teatime snack and a favourite among children.

Prep Time

20–25 minutes

Cook Time

25–30 minutes

Serves

15–20

Ingredients

4–5 green, mature but not ripe nendran/etha kaaya (Kerala bananas)

½ teaspoon turmeric powder

1 cup (150 g) powdered jaggery

½ cup (125 ml) water

½ teaspoon cardamom powder

Oil to fry

A pinch of salt

Nutritional Value

(Per serving of 25 g)

Calories: 150–180 kcal

Fat: 9–10 g

Carbohydrates: 20–25 g

Protein: 1–2 g

Fibre: 2–3 g

Sugar: 10–15 g (mainly from jaggery)

Sodium: Varies but is generally low, typically less than 10 mg

Instructions

1. Peel the bananas and keep them in a bowl of water mixed with turmeric powder for 10–15 minutes. This helps to maintain the colour and prevents them from turning brown.
2. In a separate pan, add the jaggery and water. Heat over medium heat until the jaggery melts and the mixture thickens slightly, reaching a custard-like consistency. Add a pinch of salt and cardamom powder to the syrup. Stir well. Keep aside.
3. Pat the bananas dry. Cut them into 1 cm slices and further into half-moons. Keep these pieces soaked in water to avoid discolouration.
4. Heat oil in a pan on a medium flame.
5. Pat dry the banana pieces and gently slide them into the oil, which must be hot but not smoking. With the help of a slotted ladle stir the banana pieces gently, making sure they do not stick to each other, until they turn crisp and golden-brown.
6. Remove the fried banana chips from the oil and immediately dip them into the jaggery syrup. Make sure each chip is well-coated with the syrup and separated from the other chips.
7. Place the jaggery-coated banana chips on a plate or parchment paper to cool and harden. Once they have cooled, store them in an airtight container.

Chenna Varuthatha

Yam Fry

An interesting snack made with the not-very-popular yam (jhimikhand/elephant foot). It is an ideal snack with cocktails, and makes an equally delicious and exotic accompaniment at meals.

Prep Time	**Cook Time**	**Serves**
20–25 minutes	15–20 minutes	12–15

Ingredients

250 g yam, peeled

½ teaspoon + ½ teaspoon turmeric powder

½ teaspoon chilli powder

Salt to taste

Oil to pan-fry

Nutritional Value

(Per serving of 4–6 pieces or 25 g)

Calories: 30–40 kcal

Fat: 0–1 g (depending on the amount of oil used for frying)

Carbohydrates: 6–8 g

Fibre: 1–2 g

Sugar: <1 g

Protein: <1 g

Sodium: Minimal, typically less than 10 mg

Instructions

1. Wash, peel and slice the yam into thin squares or rectangles (2.5–4 cm long, and around 2 mm thick). Leave the pieces in turmeric water for 10–15 minutes. Drain and wash well in running water. This removes the juices that tend to affect some people's throats. Use gloves if possible while cutting and washing to prevent hands from feeling itchy.
2. Pat dry the yam slices and transfer to a mixing bowl.
3. Combine the yam slices with turmeric powder, red chilli powder and salt. Mix well to coat the yam slices evenly with the spices.
4. Heat some oil in a flat, heavy-bottomed pan or skillet.
5. Add the yam slices to the pan, placing them in a single layer.
6. Fry the slices on medium flame, turning them occasionally, until they are golden brown and crispy on both sides. This may take 10–15 minutes.
7. Remove the fried yam pieces and place them on paper towels to remove excess oil.
8. Serve warm.

Naranga Achar

Lime Pickle

Also known as naranga uplithatha, it is a must in an Onam sadhya. While many bottled versions are available it can easily be made at home. Pickles were a regular part of my home meals, and I always remember images of cut lime and chilli paste being mixed together in the kitchen and a very pungent, enticing aroma filling the house.

Prep Time	**Cook Time**	**Serves**
40–45 minutes	20–25 minutes	25–30

Ingredients

10–12 medium-sized lemons

1 tablespoon mustard seeds

50 g ginger, finely chopped

4–5 green chillies, slit

2–3 sprigs curry leaves

2 teaspoons red chilli powder (adjust to taste)

¼ teaspoon asafoetida (hing)

2–3 teaspoons salt (adjust to taste)

½ cup sesame oil

1–2 tablespoons vinegar, optional (adjust to taste)

Sugar (optional, as per taste)

Nutritional Value

(Per serving of 25 g)

Calories: 30–40 kcal

Fat: 2–3 g

Carbohydrates: 2–4 g

Fibre: <1 g

Sugar: <1 g

Protein: <1 g

Sodium: Varies but can be relatively high due to the salt content, typically 300–500 mg

Instructions

1. Steam the washed lemons in a steamer for 10–15 minutes so that the skin becomes soft. Make sure it does not crack.
2. Dry the lemons thoroughly and allow to cool.
3. Cut the limes into quarters or eighths, removing any seeds.
4. Sun-dry the limes for a day or two to remove all moisture, or microwave them for a couple of minutes to save time.
5. Heat the oil and splutter the mustard seeds. Add the ginger, green chillies and curry leaves. Sauté for a minute. Lower the flame.
6. Add the red chilli powder, asafoetida and salt. Mix well.
7. Add the lime pieces and thoroughly coat them with the mixture.
8. In a pan heat the oil up to smoking point. Take it off the heat and let it cool slightly.
9. Pour the warm oil to the lime mixture and mix well.
10. Taste and adjust the salt. Red chilli powder could be added to make it more pungent. Vinegar and sugar can be added to make it tangier or sweeter.
11. Bottle the mixture and leave it in a cool, dark place for at least a week before using.

Manga Kari

Mango Pickle

Raw mangoes are a treat. During the mango season, us children were always on the lookout for raw mangoes. The fun was in stealing them from neighbours' compounds, or shooting them down with catapults. During pickling season when the raw mangoes came home, the task was easier. A couple were always given to us to keep us away from the kitchen where they were being cut. Of course, we would also volunteer to help and keep popping pieces into our mouth.

Prep Time	**Cook Time**	**Serves**
20–25 minutes	10–15 minutes	20–25

Ingredients

3–4 medium-sized raw mangoes

1–2 teaspoon mustard seeds

½ teaspoon fenugreek seeds

1–2 teaspoon red chilli powder (adjust to your spice preference)

½ teaspoon turmeric powder

½ teaspoon asafoetida

Salt to taste

4–6 tablespoons oil (preferably gingelly oil)

2–3 sprigs curry leaves (optional)

Nutritional value

(Per serving of 25 g)

Calories: 25–35 kcal

Fat: 2–3 g

Carbohydrates: 2–4 g

Fibre: <1 g

Sugar: <1 g

Protein: <1 g

Sodium: Varies but can be relatively high due to the salt content, typically around 300–500 mg

Instructions

1. Wash and thoroughly dry the mangoes.
2. Cut them into small, bite-sized pieces, discarding the seed. Ensure that the mango pieces are completely dry to prevent the pickle from spoiling.
3. Dry roast the mustard seeds and fenugreek seeds until they turn slightly brown and release their aroma. Remove from the heat and allow them to cool.
4. Grind the roasted mustard seeds and fenugreek seeds into a fine powder.
5. In a mixing bowl, combine the mango pieces, red chilli powder, turmeric powder, asafoetida, salt and the ground mustard–fenugreek powder.
6. Heat the gingelly oil up to smoking point. Allow it to cool slightly.
7. Pour the warm gingelly oil over the mango mixture and mix well. Ensure that the oil coats all the mango pieces evenly.
8. Add the curry leaves, if using, to the pickle mixture and mix again.
9. The pickle is ready to use. Store it in a bottle and let it remain for a couple of days in a cool, dark place. This will make it tastier.

Pulli Inji

Tamarind–Ginger Pickle

Pulli inji, also known as inji pulli or tamarind–ginger chutney, is another essential accompaniment of an Onam sadhya. It is also a popular condiment known for its sweet and tangy flavour. 'Pulli' in Malayalam refers to tamarind and 'inji' means ginger.

Prep Time

30 minutes

Cook Time

20–25 minutes

Serves

10–12

Ingredients

50 g tamarind

50 g ginger

50 g jaggery

2–3 green chillies (adjust to taste)

¼ teaspoon turmeric powder

¼ teaspoon red chilli powder

½ teaspoon mustard seeds

¼ teaspoon fenugreek seeds

1 sprig curry leaves

2–3 tablespoons oil

Salt to taste

Nutritional Value

(Per serving of 20–25 g/1 tablespoon)

Calories: 50–60 kcal

Fat: 1–2 g

Carbohydrates: 11–13 g

Fibre: 1–2 g

Sugar: 8–10 g

Protein: 0–1 g

Sodium: 50–100 mg

Instructions

1. Soak the tamarind in 1 cup (250 ml) of warm water for 20–30 minutes to soften it. After soaking, extract the tamarind pulp and discard any seeds or fibres.
2. Grate or finely chop the ginger.
3. Chop the green chillies fine.
4. Crush the jaggery, or grate it, and keep aside.
5. Heat oil in a pan or kadai over medium heat. Add mustard seeds and fenugreek seeds. Let them splutter.
6. Add the chopped green chillies and curry leaves. Sauté for a minute.
7. Add the grated/chopped ginger and sauté for another 2–3 minutes until the ginger becomes fragrant and slightly golden.
8. Add the tamarind pulp, turmeric powder, red chilli powder and stir well. Bring to boil and simmer until the mixture thickens.
9. Add jaggery to the tamarind mixture and stir until it dissolves completely. Adjust the amount of jaggery according to your taste. You can add more if you prefer it sweeter. Depending on how sweet, tangy or pungent you want it, adjust the quantities of the jaggery, tamarind and chillies.
10. Season with salt to taste and continue to cook, stirring occasionally, until the mixture thickens and reaches a thick, chutney-like, pourable consistency.
11. Remove it from the heat and let it cool. You can store the pulli inji in an airtight container in the refrigerator.

Inji Thayir

Ginger–Curd Relish

A simple but extraordinary dish in which ginger, chillies and curd come together as a soothing accompaniment to a sadhya. It combines the tangy and creamy goodness of yogurt, the robust flavours of ginger and the pungent kick of chillies.

Prep Time

30 minutes

Cook Time

20–25 minutes

Serves

10–12

Ingredients

200 g yogurt/curd

20–30 g fresh ginger

1–2 green chillies

Salt to taste

Nutritional Value

(Per serving of 25 g/1 tablespoon)

Calories: 50–60 kcal

Fat: 0.8–1 g

Carbohydrates: 10–12 g

Fibre: Minimal

Sugar: 1–1.5 g

Protein: 1–2 g

Sodium: 10–20 mg

Instructions

1. Grate or finely chop the fresh ginger.
2. Finely chop the green chillies.
3. Whisk the yogurt until smooth and creamy. Add salt to taste and mix well.
4. Mix the whisked yogurt, ginger and green chillies well
5. Refrigerate the mixture for at least an hour before serving to allow the flavours to meld. Inji thayir is typically served chilled.

Sambaram

Buttermilk

As a child I never drank the sambaram served at a sadhya. I would rather save that space in my stomach for an extra helping of payasam. But over the years I realised that sambaram serves as a good palate cleanser. It is quite different from the lassi you find in North India, which is thicker and has cream added to it. Sambaram basically involves whisked curd, green chilli, ginger and curry leaves.

Prep Time

5 minutes

Cook Time

5–10 minutes

Serves

4–6

Ingredients

400 ml plain yogurt/curd

Water as required

1–2 green chillies, chopped

5 cm ginger, grated

1 sprig curry leaves

Salt to taste

Nutritional Value

(Per serving of 150 ml)

Calories: 30–40 kcal

Fat: 1–2 g

Carbohydrates: 2–3 g

Fibre: Negligible

Sugar: 2–3 g

Protein: 2–3 g

Sodium: 200–300 mg

Instructions

1. In a mixing bowl, whisk the plain yogurt until smooth.
2. Add as much water as required for the desired consistency, while whisking well. You will need around 150 ml of water.
3. Add the chopped chillies, grated ginger, curry leaves and salt to the whisked yogurt. Mix well or blend lightly in a mixer.
4. Taste and adjust the seasoning, adding more salt or green chillies if needed.
5. Chill before serving.

CURRIES

When we think of a curry we usually think of ingredients cooked in a gravy. The curries in an Onam sadhya are not all gravy-like or liquid in consistency. Looking at the spread on the banana leaf, left to right, you will see a gentle progression from dry to liquid, a variation in textures.

With just four vegetables (yellow and white pumpkin, green banana, yam), coconut, green chilli, cumin and curd you can pretty much make five curries: avial, kaalan, erissery, olan (with the addition of red lobia) and the base for pulissery. The basic paste used in most of these dishes is a chutney of coconut, green chilli and cumin. The difference lies in texture and consistency. Avial has a rough, dry texture; kaalan is a very thick smooth paste with sour curd; pulissery is smooth and watery with the addition of curd; erissery is a thick paste with the added flavour and texture of grated browned coconut; while olan uses only the milk of coconut. And this makes all the difference. Each dish takes on a distinct taste, flavour and texture.

Some of the curries do not originate in Kerala but have been assimilated and become essential in a sadhya today, especially sambar. According to Venugopal Paliath the essential dishes for a Nair sadhya are kaalan, olan, erissery, a thoran, a couple of accompaniments (like chips, pickles and pulli inji), a payasam or two, and perhaps avial, the origin of which is disputed. The rest are extras added to make the sadhya more elaborate and as a show of prosperity.

Parippu

Lentil Curry

In our house the parippu served at the start of a sadhya is plain, cooked toor dal with a drizzle of ghee on top. In some parts of Kerala, it is mixed with a coconut paste and made into a curry.

Prep Time	**Cook Time**	**Serves**
5 minutes	20–25 minutes	4–6

Ingredients

100 g toor dal (split pigeon peas)

250–500 ml water

1 pinch turmeric powder

Salt to taste

Ghee to drizzle

Nutritional Value

(Per serving of 1 tablespoon, around 15 g)

Calories: 35–40 kcal

Fat: 0.5–1 g

Carbohydrates: 6–8 g

Fibre: 2–3 g

Sugar: Negligible

Protein: 2–3 g

Sodium: 50–100 mg (can vary based on salt added)

Instructions

1. Rinse the toor dal thoroughly under running water until the water runs clear.
2. In a saucepan or pressure cooker, add the washed toor dal, a pinch of turmeric and 250 ml (for pressure cooker) or 500 ml of water (for a saucepan).
3. Cook the dal until it becomes soft and mushy. If using a pressure cooker, it usually takes 2–3 whistles, or 10 minutes on a low flame after full pressure. If using a regular saucepan, it might take 20–25 minutes.
4. Once the dal is cooked and soft, mash it using the back of a spoon or a masher to achieve a smooth consistency. Add hot water if necessary.
5. Season the dal with salt to taste. Start with a small amount and adjust to your preference.

Avial

Vegetables in Coconut Chutney

Avial comes with a rich and fascinating legend. There are many stories attributed to its origin.

According to one of them, Bhima, one of the five Pandava brothers from the Indian epic Mahabharata, is believed to have invented this dish. But in Kerala there is another popular story from the royal tharavads of Kochi. The Namboodris had brought brahmin priests from Udupi to Kochi to perform pujas at temples, and a large population of people from Udupi had settled there. The king later allotted them land and quarters. Many of these people began cooking and setting up eateries in the region. Once, the king asked his cook, a brahmin from Udupi, to cook something different for a special guest whom he had invited. Faced with the challenge, the cook looked at the vegetables at his disposal: pumpkin, bananas, yam and fresh string beans. There were coconuts as well. To show off his skill he put the four vegetables together, cutting them in a different way, not small but finger-length pieces, and cooked them with a simple coconut chutney.

The name 'avial' is derived from the word 'aavi' which means 'steam'. This name reflects the cooking method used in making avial, where the vegetables are steamed or boiled and then simmered in a coconut and yogurt sauce.

Over time, avial has evolved, and various regional variations exist. Different communities and households may have their own unique ways of preparing it, using locally available vegetables and spices. However, the core elements of coconut, yogurt and mixed vegetables remain consistent in most avial recipes.

The existence of various stories that point towards the origin of this dish is perhaps why it is often referred to as a mishmash of vegetables. There are many permutations and combinations including the inclusion of vegetables like carrot and peas which is a no-no for a purist.

Going by the story from the Kochi royal kitchen, here is a traditional Nair recipe for avial.

Ingredients

100 g yellow pumpkin

100 g ash gourd

100 g raw bananas

100 g yam/string beans

1½ cups (around 150 g) grated coconut

1–2 green chillies

1 teaspoon cumin seeds

½ teaspoon turmeric powder

200 ml sour curd

2 sprigs curry leaves

1 tablespoon coconut oil

Salt to taste

Nutritional Value

(Per serving of 100–150 g)

Calories: 160–200 kcal

Fat: 10–12 g

Carbohydrates: 15–20 g

Fibre: 4–6 g

Sugar: 4–6 g

Protein: 3–5 g

Sodium: 300–400 mg (may vary based on salt content)

Instructions

1. Skin, clean and chop the vegetables into 5 cm finger-sized pieces.
2. For the raw bananas and yam, soak the pieces in turmeric water for 10–15 minutes then wash them in running water. This removes a sticky paste that could lead to a scratchy throat. Wear gloves if you can.
3. Boil each of the vegetables separately, with salt and a pinch of turmeric. Make sure the pieces are just cooked and still firm to the touch. It is important that they do not break down.
4. Make a coarse paste of the grated coconut with chillies, cumin seeds, turmeric and curd. Add some water if required to get a thick consistency.
5. In a large pan placed over medium heat, combine the coconut paste and vegetables. Simmer, stirring gently, for about 5 minutes. Remove from heat.
6. Stir in the curry leaf sprigs and top with coconut oil before serving.

If the curd is not sour enough, add a bit of tamarind or aamchur while grinding the coconut paste. It is important that the avial has a bit of tanginess.

Erissery

Pumpkin Curry

Erissery has its origins in Kerala and is associated with the legend of Mahabali. It is said to be one of the special dishes made to welcome the demon king when he visits his people during Onam. It is popularly believed that no matter how many dishes you make, without erissery the Onam sadhya is incomplete.

It is again one of those dishes that involve a lot of right timing. The pumpkin and red lobia need to be just cooked, so that when gently pressed between the thumb and forefinger they can be mashed. The grated coconut, which is browned for the garnish, has to be stirred continuously and removed from the fire before it begins to smoke and turn black.

Prep Time	**Cook Time**	**Serves**
15–20 minutes	30–60 minutes	4–6

Ingredients

250 g yellow pumpkin

125 g red lobia

1 cup (around 100 g) + ½ cup grated coconut

2–3 green chillies

½ teaspoon + ½ teaspoon turmeric powder

1–2 dry red chillies

½ teaspoon mustard seeds

1 sprig curry leaves

Oil for tempering

Salt to taste

Nutritional Value

(Per serving of 100–150 g)

Calories: 150–200 kcal

Fat: 5–10 g

Carbohydrates: 20–30 g

Fibre: 5–8 g

Sugar: 2–4 g

Protein: 5–8 g

Sodium: 200–300 mg (may vary based on salt content)

Instructions

1. Skin the pumpkin. Cut it into 2.5 cm cubes.
2. Cook the pumpkin with ½ teaspoon turmeric, salt and enough water till well-cooked (20–25 minutes). The pieces should be soft when a piece is pressed between your thumb and forefinger.
3. While the pumpkin cooks, prepare the red lobia. It is preferable to soak it for a couple of hours. Pressure cook for 2–3 whistles or about 10 minutes on a low flame after pressure builds. You could also slow-cook it in a saucepan with enough water till well done (30–45 minutes). Again, the lobia should be soft when a piece is pressed between your thumb and forefinger.
4. Grind 1 cup of coconut with green chilli, ½ teaspoon turmeric and enough water to make a coarse paste.
5. Dry roast the other ½ cup grated coconut till brown. Keep stirring on a low flame and remove from fire before it smokes or turns black. Keep aside.
6. Mix together the coconut paste, cooked red lobia and pumpkin on a low flame for about 5 minutes. Mash the pumpkin lightly. It should not become a paste but just crumble so that the pieces are still visible.
7. In a tempering pan heat some oil, crackle mustard seeds, dry red chillies and curry leaves and pour over the pumpkin mixture and mix.
8. The browned coconut can be mixed with the pumpkin mixture or used as a garnish before serving, sprinkled over the top.

Kaalan

Yam and Raw Banana Curry

This is another must in an Onam sadhya. The story behind kaalan is linked to a mythical tale involving the demon king Mahabali. It is said that when Mahabali granted a boon to a young brahmin boy, the boy requested a dish that combined sour, sweet and spicy flavours. Kaalan, with its combination of yogurt, yam, raw bananas and coconut, is believed to be a representation of this special dish.

Kaalan is one of the touchstones of a good sadhya. As soon as it is served, connoisseurs of a sadhya run a finger through the curry and gently press it on the yam pieces. The curry has to be smooth in texture, and the yam should just about crumble. Then comes the taste test, a quick lick of the fingers which would result in either an enthusiastic look or a despondent one. The flavour has to be a perfect balance between tangy and pungent, with just a hint of sweetness and sourness.

It took me many, many years to strike the right balance before my mother actually approved my preparation. I must admit that when the curd is not sour enough, I resort to adding a pinch of aamchur, a trick I revealed to my mother much later after her approval.

Ingredients

250 g yam

150 g (1–2) raw bananas

1 cup (around 100 g) coconut

1 cup (around 200 g) yogurt/curd

1 teaspoon cumin seeds

1–2 green chillies

Turmeric powder as required

Salt to taste

Oil for tempering

½ teaspoon mustard seeds

1–2 dried red chillies

1 sprig curry leaves

Nutritional Value

(Per serving of 100–150 g)

Calories: 150–200 kcal

Fat: 8–10 g

Carbohydrates: 15–20 g

Fibre: 3–5 g

Sugar: 2–4 g

Protein: 3–5 g

Sodium: 200–300 mg (may vary based on salt content)

Instructions

1. Skin the yam, lightly peel the raw bananas and cut them into 2.5 cm cubes. Soak them separately in turmeric water for 10–15 minutes. Wash well in running water (this removes the juice that tends to irritate the throat). Preferably use a pair of gloves while handling the yam and bananas.
2. Cook the yam and bananas separately in enough water and a pinch of turmeric. The bananas will cook in about 10 minutes and the yam in 15–20 minutes.
3. Meanwhile, whisk the sour yogurt to a smooth consistency.
4. Grate the coconut with green chillies, cumin seeds and a pinch of turmeric to a smooth, thick paste, adding water as required.
5. Combine the coconut mixture with the curd and place on a medium flame. Stir continuously for about 5 minutes. The mixture should reach boiling point.
6. Add the cooked yam and banana. Mix well and cook for a few minutes. Remove from heat.
7. Heat oil in a tempering pan. Crackle mustard seeds, red chillies and curry leaves. Pour over the curry and mix.

Olan

Ash Gourd and String Beans Stew

Olan is a mild curry with coconut milk, and its origins are often traced back to the Syrian Christian community in Kerala, given that it is similar to the stew prepared by them. The simplicity of its preparation allows the natural flavours of the ash gourd and the fresh string beans to come through along with the creamy texture of the coconut milk.

Prep Time

30 minutes

Cook Time

15–20 minutes

Serves

4–6

Ingredients

250 g ash gourd/white pumpkin

150 g string beans/green lobia (or 150 g of cooked red lobia)

½ cup thin (second) coconut milk + 1 cup thick (first) coconut milk (or 200 ml coconut milk and 150 ml water)

1–2 green chillies, slit

1 sprig curry leaves

1 tablespoon oil (preferably coconut oil)

Salt to taste

Nutritional Value

(Per serving of 100–150 g)

Calories: 120–150 kcal

Fat: 6–8 g

Carbohydrates: 12–15 g

Fibre: 3–4 g

Sugar: 2–4 g

Protein: 2–3 g

Sodium: 200–300 mg (may vary based on salt content)

Instructions

1. Skin the pumpkin and cut into thin slices.
2. String the beans and cut into 2.5 cm pieces.
3. In a pan heat the coconut oil. Sauté the green chillies. Add the pumpkin and string beans. Sauté for a minute. Add the thin coconut milk to cover the vegetables. You could alternatively use the same quantity of water. Cook till the vegetables are tender. It will take around 10 minutes. If using cooked red lobia instead of the string beans, add it to the pumpkin after it is cooked.
4. If using freshly made coconut milk, add the thick coconut milk. Or add the coconut milk packet. Simmer for a few minutes.
5. Add the curry leaf sprig and take off the heat.
6. Drizzle a bit of coconut oil over it before serving.

Kootu Kari

Mixed Vegetable and Chickpea Curry

The preparation of kootu kari is associated with the ritual of offering food to the deity during festivals. It symbolises the coming together of various elements to create a harmonious and flavourful dish. The dish is believed to have originated as a way to celebrate the harvest season as it incorporates a variety of locally available vegetables. It typically includes a mix of vegetables such as yam, raw banana, gourds and black chickpeas. These ingredients are commonly grown in Kerala and are readily available during the harvest season.

Prep Time	**Cook Time**	**Serves**
10–15 minutes	15–20 minutes	4–6

Ingredients

125 g black chickpeas (kadla/kala chana)

100 g yam

100 g or 1 medium-sized raw banana

100 g snake gourd/yellow pumpkin

1 cup (around 100 g) grated coconut

1–2 green chillies

½ teaspoon cumin seeds

½ teaspoon black pepper

2.5 cm piece ginger

1 sprig curry leaves

Salt to taste

Turmeric powder as required

Water as required

For seasoning

2 tablespoons oil (preferably coconut oil)

½ teaspoon mustard seeds

1–2 dried red chillies

1 pinch asafoetida

Nutritional Value

(Per serving of 100–150 g)

Calories: 150–200 kcal

Fat: 6–8 g

Carbohydrates: 20–25 g

Fibre: 4–6 g

Sugar: 2–4 g

Protein: 4–6 g

Sodium: 200–300 mg (may vary based on salt content)

Instructions

1. Soak the black chickpeas overnight.
2. Drain the soaked black chickpeas and pressure cook them with enough water until they are soft and cooked. After one whistle, reduce heat and simmer for 15–20 minutes. Set aside to cool. If you are not using a pressure cooker, cover the black chickpeas with enough water and cook over the stovetop. Bring to a boil. Lower heat, cover and allow to simmer till the chickpeas are cooked. It will take around 1 hour or more.
3. In a blender, combine the grated coconut, green chillies, cumin seeds, ginger, turmeric powder, peppercorns and a little water.
4. Blend until you get a smooth paste.
5. Peel and cut yam into 2.5 cm cubes. Soak them in turmeric water for 10–15 minutes. Wash well in running water. This removes the juice that tends to irritate the throat. Preferably use gloves to avoid itchy hands.
6. Similarly, peel and cube the raw bananas.
7. Peel and cube the snake gourd/pumpkin, removing the seeds.
8. Cook the vegetables separately with a pinch of turmeric and salt to taste. The yam will take 15–20 minutes, the raw banana around 10 minutes and the snake gourd/pumpkin around 15 minutes. The vegetables should be tender but not mushy. Drain any excess water.
9. In a pan over medium heat, add the cooked black chickpeas, vegetables and coconut paste. Add salt if required. Mix well.
10. In a tempering pan, heat coconut oil over medium heat. Add mustard seeds and let them splutter. Add dried red chillies, curry leaves and a pinch of asafoetida. Sauté for a minute. Pour this seasoning over the kootu curry and mix well.

Vellarikai Pulissery

Cucumber Curd Curry

This is a yogurt-based dish with the addition of ground coconut. It is not very different from a kaalan. During the mango season, pulissery is made with ripe mangoes, giving the dish a sweet and sour flavour. Pineapple is another popular fruit used in pulissery, and another variation is with ash gourd. My clientele in Delhi refer to it as the Kerala raita.

Prep Time

10–15 minutes

Cook Time

15–20 minutes

Serves

4–6

Ingredients

250 g 'desi' yellow cucumber or regular cucumbers

1 cup (75–100 g) grated coconut

1–2 green chillies

1 teaspoon cumin seeds

1 cup (around 200 g) plain curd

Water as required

½ teaspoon mustard seeds

1–2 dried red chillies

¼ teaspoon fenugreek seeds

1 sprig curry leaves

Nutritional value

(Per serving of 150–200 g)

Calories: 70–100 kcal

Fat: 3–5 g

Carbohydrates: 7–10 g

Fibre: 1–2 g

Sugar: 3–5 g

Protein: 2–4 g

Sodium: 200–300 mg (may vary based on salt content)

Instructions

1. Skin the cucumber(s) and chop into 2.5 cm cubes. Remove seeds if they are very large and ripe.
2. Boil the cucumber pieces with just enough water till cooked. It will take 10–15 minutes. Keep aside.
3. Whisk the curd well.
4. Grind the coconut to a smooth paste along with green chillies, cumin seeds and enough water to get a thick, pourable consistency.
5. Add the coconut mixture to the whisked curd. Mix well along with the cooked cucumber.
6. Place the mixture on a low flame, stirring continuously till it comes to a boil. Remove from heat.
7. In a tempering pan, heat some oil. Crackle the mustard seeds, dried red chillies, fenugreek seeds and curry leaves. Add to the cucumber mixture.

For mango pulissery use 2 ripe mangoes. For pineapple pulissery use around 1 cup chopped pineapple. For ash gourd pulissery use 250 g ash gourd. Boil the vegetables the same way as the cucumber.

Ulli Theeyal

Shallot Curry

Ulli refers to pearl onions and theeyal literally means 'burnt', referring to the process of roasting coconut almost to a burnt state. It may look like a very dark-coloured sambar but it is quite different, especially in the use of coconut and the cooking method. The colour of the theeyal comes from roasting the coconut to a dark, golden-brown colour and sautéing onions to a dark brown colour. It is a rich, tangy and slightly sweet curry.

Prep Time

15–20 minutes

Cook Time

45–90 minutes

Serves

4–6

Ingredients

For roasting and grinding

75–100 g grated coconut

1 teaspoon coriander seeds

½ teaspoon cumin seeds

½ teaspoon fenugreek seeds

2–4 dried red chillies (adjust to your spice preference)

½ teaspoon turmeric powder

1 tablespoon tamarind dissolved in 250 ml water (or juice from one large lemon-sized ball of tamarind soaked in 250 ml water for 10 minutes, squeezed and sieved)

For the gravy

250 g shallots (small onions), peeled and kept whole

2 tablespoons oil (preferably coconut oil)

½ teaspoon mustard seeds

½ teaspoon fenugreek seeds

1 sprig curry leaves

2–3 green chillies, slit

½ teaspoon asafoetida

Salt to taste

Water as needed

Nutritional Value

(Per serving of 100–150 g)

Calories: 150–200 kcal

Fat: 12–15 g

Carbohydrates: 10–15 g

Fibre: 2–3 g

Sugar: 2–3 g

Protein: 2–3 g

Sodium: 200–300 mg (can vary depending on salt added)

Instructions

1. Heat a pan on medium-low heat and dry roast the grated coconut until it turns dark brown, almost black. Stir continuously to avoid burning. Keep aside to cool.
2. In the same pan, dry roast coriander seeds, cumin seeds, fenugreek seeds and dried red chillies until the spices release their aroma. Allow to cool.
3. In a blender, add the coconut, spice mixture, turmeric and water as required to get a smooth paste.
4. Heat the oil in a heavy-bottomed pan or kadai over medium heat. Add mustard seeds and let them splutter. Then add fenugreek seeds, curry leaves, green chillies and asafoetida. Sauté for a minute.
5. Add the peeled onions (ulli) to the pan and sauté them for 5–7 minutes until they become translucent and browned (this browning also helps in giving the curry a dark colour). Stir occasionally.
6. Reduce the heat to low and add the ground coconut–spice paste. Mix well and sauté for another 5–7 minutes, stirring continuously. The mixture should turn dark brown and fragrant.
7. Add salt to taste and continue cooking for a few more minutes.
8. Pour enough water to cover the shallots and bring the mixture to a boil. Then, reduce the heat to low, cover and simmer for 20–25 minutes until the shallots are tender and the gravy thickens. Stir occasionally and add more water if needed to achieve your desired consistency.

Sambar

Vegetables and Lentil Curry

While there are various legends and tales associated with the creation of sambar, the most widely accepted version attributes its origin to the royal Maratha courts in Thanjavur. Some attribute it to the king himself and some to his chef. The dish was built upon the Maharashtrian amti, a dal preparation with hardly any spices or vegetables. Either the king found the dal very insipid and in the absence of his chef added ingredients to 'liven' it up a bit, or when asked by the king to cook something different than the usual dal, the chef himself enhanced it with a spice powder and vegetables. The dish is so versatile that every region – in fact, almost every household – has its own version of sambar. Here is the recipe from my tharavad, a largely accepted version served at Nair Onam sadhyas.

Prep Time	Cook Time	Serves
15–20 minutes	45–60 minutes	4–6

Ingredients

For the sambar powder

2 teaspoons coriander seeds

1 teaspoon chana dal

1 teaspoon urad dal

1 teaspoon cumin seeds

½ teaspoon fenugreek seeds

2–3 dried red chillies (adjust to preference)

1 pinch asafoetida

½ teaspoon black peppercorns

½ teaspoon turmeric powder

For sambar

120 g toor dal (split pigeon peas), washed and soaked for 30 minutes

250 g mixed vegetables (drumsticks, pumpkin, shallots, brinjal and/or any other local vegetables you prefer), cleaned and chopped

1 onion, chopped

2–3 green chillies, slit

½ teaspoon asafoetida

1 teaspoon mustard seeds

A few curry leaves

2 tablespoons oil

Salt to taste

Water as needed

1 tablespoon tamarind paste or a lime-sized piece of tamarind

Nutritional Value

(Per serving of 100–150 g)

Calories: 100–150 kcal

Fat: 2 g

Carbohydrates: 15–20 g

Fibre: 3–5 g

Sugar: 2–3 g

Protein: 4–6 g

Sodium: 300–600 mg (depends on the salt added)

Instructions

1. Heat a pan over medium heat and add all the ingredients for the sambar powder except turmeric. Dry roast them until they turn aromatic and slightly golden-brown. Be careful not to burn them. Let the roasted spices cool, and then grind them into a fine powder along with turmeric. This is your sambar powder.
2. If not using tamarind paste, soak the tamarind in ½ cup warm water for about 20 minutes to soften it. Squeeze the tamarind to extract the juice, and discard the pulp and seeds. Set the tamarind extract aside.
3. Cook the dal with a pinch of turmeric in a pressure cooker with 250 ml water. After one whistle, lower the flame and let it simmer for 10–15 minutes. Allow to cool. Or cook it over the stovetop in a vessel with a pinch of turmeric and 500 ml water. It will take around 30 minutes.
4. Let the dal cool. Mash it and keep aside.
5. In a large pot, add the chopped mixed vegetables, onion, green chillies and enough water to cover them. Cook the vegetables until they are tender but not mushy, 15–20 minutes.
6. Now, to the above, add the cooked and mashed toor dal. Mix everything well.
7. Add the homemade sambar powder (there will be 2–3 tablespoons) and salt. Stir to combine all the ingredients.
8. Add the tamarind paste/extract, bring to a boil and cook for a few minutes until the raw smell of tamarind disappears.
9. Adjust the consistency by adding water as needed.
10. Bring to a boil and then lower the flame and let the sambar simmer for 10–15 minutes.
11. In a tempering pan, heat a little oil, add mustard seeds and curry leaves. Once they splutter, pour this seasoning over the sambar.

Boil the vegetables along with the sambar powder. I find using this method allows the vegetables to soak in flavours of the powder better. This is a tip I learnt from my mother.

Rasam

Lentil Soup

The word 'rasam' itself is derived from the Sanskrit word 'rasa', which means juice or extract, indicating its liquid nature. Rasam is known for its unique blend of flavours, often incorporating ingredients like tamarind, with or without tomatoes, spices and aromatic herbs like curry leaves. It has been considered a comfort food, a digestive aid and a remedy for various ailments. Rasam is also an integral part of South Indian festivals, weddings and special occasions, where it is served as a welcoming and comforting drink. Over the years, rasam has evolved, and numerous regional variations and recipes have emerged, each with its unique blend of spices and ingredients. While tomato-based rasam is prevalent, there are also variations like lemon rasam, pepper rasam and pineapple rasam, among others.

This recipe for rasam is without tomatoes which were only introduced to Kerala by the Portuguese in the early sixteenth century.

Prep Time	**Cook Time**	**Serves**
15–20 minutes	45–60 minutes	4–6

Ingredients

For rasam powder

1 tablespoon coriander seeds

1 teaspoon cumin seeds

½ teaspoon fenugreek seeds

2–3 dried red chillies

8–10 black peppercorns

1 teaspoon toor dal (split pigeon peas)

1 teaspoon chana dal (split chickpeas)

5–6 curry leaves

For rasam

125 g toor dal

1 lemon-sized ball or 1 tablespoon tamarind paste

2.5 cm piece ginger, crushed and chopped

½ teaspoon turmeric powder

1 teaspoon jaggery/sugar jaggery/sugar (optional)

1–2 tablespoon oil

½ teaspoon mustard seeds

½ teaspoon cumin seeds

2–3 dried red chillies

1 pinch asafoetida

1 sprig curry leaves

Coriander leaves to garnish

Nutritional value

(Per serving of 100–150 ml)

Calories: 15–20 kcal

Fat: 1 g

Carbohydrates: 3–4 g

Fibre: 1 g

Sugar: 1 g

Protein: 1–2 g

Sodium: 200–500 mg (depends on the quantity of salt used)

Instructions

For the powder

1. Heat a dry pan over low-medium heat. Add coriander seeds, cumin seeds, fenugreek seeds, torn, dried red chillies, black peppercorns, toor dal, chana dal and curry leaves to the pan.
2. Dry roast the ingredients until they become fragrant and the dals turn golden-brown. Stir frequently to avoid burning. Allow the roasted spices to cool completely, then grind them into a fine powder.

For the rasam

1. Cook the dal with a pinch of turmeric in a pressure cooker with 250 ml water. After one whistle, lower the flame and let it simmer for 10–15 minutes. Allow to cool. Or cook it over the stovetop in a vessel with a pinch of turmeric and 500 ml water. It will take around 30 minutes.
2. Let the dal cool. Mash it and keep aside.
3. Soak the tamarind ball in ½ cup warm water for about 15 minutes. Squeeze the tamarind to extract the pulp. Strain the tamarind extract into a bowl and discard any solids. Or use tamarind paste dissolved in ½ cup warm water.
4. In a large pot, combine the cooked toor dal, turmeric powder, ginger, tamarind water, jaggery or sugar (if using) and salt. Add 4–5 cups of water and bring to a boil. Simmer for about 10 minutes.
5. Stir in the prepared rasam powder. Adjust salt. Simmer for a few more minutes.
6. In a tempering pan, heat ghee over medium heat. Add mustard seeds and cumin seeds. When they splutter, add dried red chillies, asafoetida and curry leaves. Sauté for a few seconds until fragrant. Pour the tempered ghee mixture over the rasam and mix well.
7. Garnish the rasam with chopped fresh coriander leaves.

THORANS

In Kerala cuisine, thoran refers to a dry vegetable stir-fry dish that is usually made with grated or finely chopped vegetables, coconut and a tempering of spices. Nair-style thorans are known for their simplicity. They are characterised by their heavy use of coconut. Grated coconut is used not only in the dish itself but often as a garnish as well.

Thorans can be made with a wide variety of vegetables, including, but not limited to, cabbage, beans, carrots, beetroot, gourds, and even leafy greens like spinach. Each vegetable brings its own unique flavour and texture to the dish. Thorans are usually mild in terms of pungency. The focus is more on the natural flavour of the vegetable and the subtle spices used in tempering, which is an essential step. Typically, mustard seeds, cumin seeds, urad dal (split black gram), chana dal (split chickpea lentils), dried red chillies and curry leaves are used for tempering. This adds an extra layer of flavour to the dish. Thorans are garnished with freshly grated coconut just before serving. This adds a delightful freshness and contrast in texture to the dish.

Thorans can be accompaniments to rice and other curries. They are also had as a snack or light meal when paired with items like kanji (rice gruel) or appam (rice pancakes).

While the basic concept of a dry vegetable stir-fry with coconut remains, there are now countless variations to cater to different tastes and dietary preferences.

In an Onam sadhya there would be at least two to three thorans, traditionally comprising of seasonal vegetables like beetroot, string beans, cabbage, snake gourd, raw banana and yam. Today, with vegetables like beans and carrot available in abundance, thorans made from them are very popular.

Beetroot Thoran

Beetroot Stir-fry

The bright red colour of beetroot stands out on the banana leaf in a sadhya. The vegetable can be cut either into tiny pieces or grated.

Prep Time	**Cook Time**	**Serves**
10–15 minutes	25–30 minutes	4–6

Ingredients

250 g or 2 medium-sized beetroots

½ cup (around 50 g) coconut, grated

½ teaspoon mustard seeds

½ teaspoon cumin seeds

½ teaspoon urad dal

½ teaspoon chana dal

1–2 dried red chillies

A few curry leaves

1 tablespoon oil

Salt to taste

Nutritional Value

(Per serving of 2 tbsp)

Calories: 16–17 kcal

Fat: 1.3–1.4 g

Carbohydrates: 0.9–1 g

Fibre: 0.6–0.7 g

Sugar: 0.9–1 g

Protein: 0.4–0.5 g

Sodium: 200–400 mg (depends on the salt added)

Instructions

1. Peel the beetroot and parboil it for 10–15 minutes in boiling water. Let it cool.
2. Grate or chop into small cubes. Set aside.
3. Heat the oil in a deep skillet or pan over medium heat. Add mustard seeds and let them splutter. Then add cumin seeds, urad dal, chana dal, dried red chillies and curry leaves. Sauté until the dals turn golden-brown.
4. Add the grated/chopped beetroot to the pan. Add salt to taste. Mix well to combine with the tempered spices.
5. Cover the pan and further cook the beetroot on low to medium heat. Stir occasionally to ensure even cooking. Cook for 10–15 minutes or until the beetroot becomes tender. If it starts to stick to the bottom of the pan, you can sprinkle a little water.
6. Once the beetroot is cooked, add the grated coconut (save some for garnishing) and mix well.
7. Just before serving, garnish the beetroot thoran with freshly grated coconut.

Muttakose Thoran

Cabbage Stir-fry

While cabbage is not native to Kerala, it has long been a much-used vegetable. The trick in preparing a good cabbage thoran is in how finely you cut the cabbage (the finer the better) and how long you cook it (letting it remain crunchy gives the best results).

Prep Time	**Cook Time**	**Serves**
10–15 minutes	25–30 minutes	4–6

Ingredients

1 medium-sized cabbage

½ cup (around 50 g) coconut, grated

1–2 green chillies, slit

½ teaspoon mustard seeds

½ teaspoon chana dal

1 sprig curry leaves

1 tablespoon oil

Salt to taste

Nutritional Value

(Per serving of 2 tablespoons)

Calories: 5–6 kcal

Fat: 0.4–0.5 g

Carbohydrates: 0.3–0.4 g

Fibre: 0.1–0.2 g

Sugar: 0.1–0.2 g

Protein: 0.2–0.3 g

Sodium: 200–400 mg (depends on quantity of salt used)

Instructions

1. Chop the cabbage finely in strips. Wash well and let it drain in a colander.
2. Heat coconut oil in a pan and add mustard seeds and chana dal. Let this splutter.
3. Add the slit green chillies and let them get seared.
4. Add chopped cabbage and salt to taste. Sauté for a few minutes on high heat until the cabbage starts to soften. Cover and cook for a couple of minutes. Do not add water (just a sprinkling if the cabbage is very dry) or overcook the cabbage; it should remain firm and crunchy with a bite.
5. Add the grated coconut. Mix well. Garnish with curry leaves and serve.

Achinga/Payaru Thoran

String Beans Stir-fry

While today the regular French beans are popularly used for thoran, traditionally the recipe called for string beans as they were grown widely in tharavad homes. Like the other thorans, the manner of cutting the beans is important, as they need to be cut very fine, into pieces of around 2 mm. Today, with the availability of different varieties of green beans, any kind can be used.

Prep Time

10–15 minutes

Cook Time

5–10 minutes

Serves

4–6

Ingredients

250 g string beans or French beans

½ cup (around 50 g) coconut, grated

½ teaspoon mustard seeds

1–2 dried red chillies

1 sprig curry leaves

Salt to taste

1 tablespoon oil

Nutritional Value

(Per serving of 2 tablespoons)

Calories: 10–12 kcal

Fat: 0.9–1.1 g

Carbohydrates: 0.6–0.8 g

Fibre: 0.3–0.4 g

Sugar: 0.1–0.2 g

Protein: 0.4–0.5 g

Sodium: 200–400 mg (depends on the salt added)

Instructions

1. String and chop beans finely or into pieces of 1 inch. Gather a handful of beans at a time, hold together on the chopping board and slice them through at intervals of ½ cm. Wash well.
2. Heat coconut oil in a pan and add mustard seeds and torn, dried red chillies. Let this splutter.
3. Add chopped green beans. Sauté on high for a few minutes.
4. Sprinkle some water, salt to taste, mix well, cover and cook on medium heat for 5–8 minutes till the beans are just cooked and still firm and crunchy.
5. Add the grated coconut and curry leaves.
6. Mix well and serve warm.

Padavalanga Thoran

Snake Gourd Stir-fry

A seasonal and popular gourd, snake gourd gets its name from the scale-like pattern and thin, long shape of the vegetable. As children when we saw them growing in thick vegetable patches, sometimes we would mistake them for green grass snakes.

Prep Time	**Cook Time**	**Serves**
10–15 minutes	5–10 minutes	4–6

Ingredients

1 medium-sized snake gourd

½ cup (around 50 g) coconut, grated

½ teaspoon mustard seeds

½ teaspoon urad dal

1–2 dried red chillies

1 sprig curry leaves

1 tablespoon oil

Salt to taste

Nutritional Value

(Per serving of 2 tablespoons)

Calories: 10–12 kcal

Fat: 0.9–1.1 g

Carbohydrates: 0.7–0.9 g

Fibre: 0.3–0.4 g

Sugar: 0.2–0.3 g

Protein: 0.3–0.4 g

Sodium: 200–400 mg
(depends on the salt added)

Instructions

1. Peel the snake gourd. Cut it lengthwise into half and remove the pith. Cut it into thin strips and chop finely into ½ cm pieces.
2. Heat coconut oil in a pan and add mustard seeds, urad dal and torn, dried red chillies. Let them splutter.
3. Add chopped snake gourd, salt to taste. Sauté. Cover and cook for a couple of minutes.
4. Add grated coconut and curry leaves. Mix well.

Kaaya Upperi

Raw Banana Upperi

This is not exactly a thoran in that no grated coconut is used. It is left on a low flame for a while, till a certain crispiness is achieved on the outside. It is served along with the other thorans during the sadhya. It can be served on its own as a snack too.

Prep Time	**Cook Time**	**Serves**
10–15 minutes	5–10 minutes	4

Ingredients

2–3 raw green bananas

½ teaspoon turmeric

½ teaspoon mustard seeds

½ teaspoon chana dal

1–2 dried red chillies

1 sprig curry leaves

1 tablespoon oil

Salt to taste

Nutritional Value

(Per serving of 2 tablespoons)

Calories: 8–10 kcal

Fat: 0–0.1 g

Carbohydrates: 1.6–1.8 g

Fibre: 0.2–0.3 g

Sugar: 0.4–0.5 g

Protein: 0.3–0.4 g

Sodium: 200–400 mg (depends on quantity of salt used)

Instructions

1. Roughly peel the green bananas. Cut them vertically in half and further cut the halves into two pieces vertically, then chop them in 1 cm pieces. (Use gloves to avoid itchy hands.)
2. Soak them in turmeric water for 10 minutes. Wash well in running water and drain. This helps remove a paste that could cause a scratchy throat.
3. Heat oil in a pan and add mustard seeds, torn, dried red chillies, chana dal and curry leaves. Let them splutter.
4. Add the raw banana pieces and salt to taste. Sauté well for a few minutes. Sprinkle some water, mix and cover. Cook for 5–10 minutes. The bananas should be just cooked and not mushy.
5. Once cooked, allow the banana pieces to simmer on very low heat, stirring occasionally, till they become crisp on the outside. This will take 10–15 minutes.
6. Once crisp on the outside, serve warm.

Cheera Thoran

Red Spinach Stir-fry

Cheera is a seasonal variety of spinach that is very popular in Kerala and grows there in abundance. Making a thoran out of its leaves is tricky as often they turn into a mush because of the fast cooking time. A very quick stir-fry is what is called for. The fresh, white grated coconut sets off the dark red spinach very well. The addition of shallots gives it a twist.

		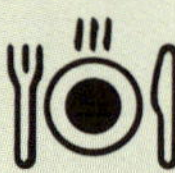
Prep Time	**Cook Time**	**Serves**
10–15 minutes	25–30 minutes	4

Ingredients

3–4 cups (250 g) red spinach leaves, chopped

½ cup (around 50 g) coconut, grated

4–6 shallots (or 1 onion)

½ teaspoon mustard seeds

½ teaspoon cumin seeds

1–2 dry red chillies

1 sprig curry leaves

Oil (for tempering)

Salt to taste

Nutritional Value

(for a serving of 2 tablespoons)

Calories: 60–80 kcal

Fat: 5–7 g

Carbohydrates: 3–5 g

Fibre: 1–2 g

Sugar: 1–2 g

Protein: 1–2 g

Sodium: 100–200 mg (depends on the salt added)

Instructions

1. Clean the red spinach thoroughly, remove any hard stems, and finely chop the leaves.
2. Finely chop the shallots and set them aside.
3. In a deep pan or kadai, heat the oil. Add mustard seeds. When they start to splutter, add cumin seeds, torn, dried red chillies and curry leaves.
4. Add the chopped shallots. Sauté until the shallots become golden-brown.
5. Add the chopped red spinach. Add salt, sprinkle some water, mix well, cover and cook for around 10 minutes. Check in between; if the leaves are very dry and sticking to the pan, sprinkle some more water.
6. Once the leaves are cooked, add the grated coconut and mix, or sprinkle the coconut on top before serving.

PAYASAMS

My father would have a special puja every Thursday night for Sai Baba and on that day my mother would make pal payasam (rice, milk and sugar). Everyone would have a bowl of it after dinner but I would keep mine aside to have next morning when it was cold. Even today, given the choice, I have my payasams cold, especially the ones made with milk or coconut milk. The semi-solid jaggery–rice payasams that use a lot of ghee tend to congeal when cold, so they need to be warmed depending on the ambient temperature.

Payasam is an integral part of an Onam sadhya. Other dishes may be skipped, but at least one, if not two, payasams are a must. They are made using ingredients like rice, rice flakes, jaggery, milk, coconut milk and lentils. The little payasam that is placed on the leaf prior to the main service is often the touchstone for connoisseurs as far as the desserts are concerned. A little touch of a finger to the payasam and a lick of it helps them judge the remaining desserts in the sadhya. It is always difficult to please these connoisseurs; the most you get out of them is a slight nod of the head – too sweet; not sweet enough; rice or dal not cooked enough or overcooked. It's difficult to please everyone.

In these payasam recipes, while I give quantities for sugar and jaggery, do begin by adding a little less, tasting and then adjusting the sweetness depending on the people being served. You are in trouble if the people are a mixed lot: some preferring very sweet and some not so sweet. In that case go by what you like. In my case it is always on the plus side. I think a payasam that is not sweet enough is almost a curry gone wrong!

Over the years and many Onam sadhyas later, I have found, thanks to my aunts who are connoisseurs, that it is always better to err on the side of more after having heard 'madram pora' (not sweet enough) too often.

Palada Payasam

Rice Flakes and Milk Dessert

'Pasta milk pudding' – that is what a foreigner once called palada payasam, a customary dessert served at many festive occasions. The ada or rice flakes were once made in homes but today they are easily available off the shelf. Given that coconut milk can also be bought in tins and tetra packs, this is a dessert that is simple to make.

Prep Time	**Cook Time**	**Serves**
10–15 minutes	60–75 minutes	4–6

Ingredients

100 g ada

1 litre full-cream milk

200 g sugar

4–5 green cardamoms

2 tablespoons ghee

8–10 cashew nuts

8–10 raisins

Nutritional Value

(Per medium bowl, around 4–6 tablespoons)

Calories: 200–250 kcal

Fat: 5–7 g

Carbohydrates: 30–40 g

Fibre: 1 g

Sugar: 10–20 g (depends on the amount of sugar used)

Protein: 3–5 g

Sodium: Negligible

Instructions

1. Wash the rice flakes in running water till they become soft.
2. Peel the cardamom and powder the seeds. Keep aside.
3. In a large, heavy-bottomed pan, bring the milk to a boil.
4. Once the milk starts boiling, reduce the heat to low and add the washed ada to the milk. Stir well to combine.
5. Allow the milk and ada mixture to simmer on low heat. Stir frequently to prevent sticking and ensure that the ada cooks evenly. Let the milk thicken, reduce by about a quarter and take on a pale yellow colour. This can take 30–40 minutes.
6. When the ada is cooked well and the mixture thickens, add the sugar. Stir well until the sugar completely dissolves. Add the crushed or powdered cardamom to the payasam. Allow to simmer for another 10 minutes.
7. While the payasam simmers, in a separate small pan, heat the ghee. Add the cashew nuts and raisins and fry them until they turn golden-brown. Make sure not to burn them. Strain the fried cashews and raisins from the ghee and add them to the payasam.
8. Allow the payasam to simmer for a few more minutes. Serve hot or chilled.

You could par-cook the ada in water before adding to the milk which has been reduced.

Ada Pradhaman

Rice Flakes, Jaggery and Coconut Milk Dessert

This is a variation of the palada payasam in that jaggery is used instead of sugar.

Prep Time

10–15 minutes

Cook Time

60–75 minutes

Serves

4–6

Ingredients

100 g ada

750 ml water

250 g jaggery

400 ml coconut milk

4–5 green cardamoms

2 tablespoons ghee

6–8 cashew nuts, broken

8–10 raisins

Nutritional Value

(Per medium bowl or 4–6 tablespoons)

Calories: 200–250 kcal

Fat: 8–12 g

Carbohydrates: 30–40 g

Fibre: 1–2 g

Sugar: 15–20 g

Protein: 3–5 g

Sodium: Negligible

Instructions

1. Wash the ada thoroughly under running water till they become soft.
2. Grate or crush the jaggery.
3. Add ½ cup water to ½ cup coconut milk to make it thin. If you are making fresh coconut milk, take 1 cup of thick milk and 1 cup of thin milk. (See Appendix 2 for making fresh coconut milk.)
4. In a saucepan, bring 2 cups of water to a boil. Add the washed rice flakes to the boiling water and cook them for 10–15 minutes or until they are just cooked. (They will be further cooked in coconut milk to soften them some more.) Drain the water and set the cooked ada aside.
5. In a separate large, heavy-bottomed pan, over medium heat, dissolve the grated or crushed jaggery in a little water and strain it to remove any impurities. Keep this jaggery syrup aside.
6. In the same pan, add the cooked ada and thin coconut milk. Cook on low heat, stirring frequently, until the ada absorbs most of the coconut milk and becomes soft. This may take 15–20 minutes.
7. Add the jaggery syrup to the ada mixture and stir well. Continue to cook on low heat until the mixture thickens and comes together. This can take another 10–15 minutes.
8. Once the ada and jaggery mixture has thickened, reduce the heat to the lowest setting and slowly pour in the thick coconut milk while stirring continuously.
9. Add the crushed or powdered cardamom for flavour and mix it in.
10. Allow the payasam to simmer for a few more minutes. Be careful not to let it boil vigorously as it can curdle.
11. In a separate small pan, heat the ghee. Add the cashew nuts and raisins and fry them until they turn golden-brown. Make sure not to burn them. Strain the fried cashews and raisins from the ghee and add them to the ada pradhaman.
12. Give the payasam a final stir and remove from heat. Ada pradhaman can be served warm or at room temperature.

Parippu Payasam

Lentil Dessert

This is a brown payasam often considered a must at an Onam sadhya. It is either the ada pradhaman or this. If you are serving the white palada payasam then it is preferable to serve this as the brown one.

Prep Time	**Cook Time**	**Serves**
5–10 minutes	30–45 minutes	4–6

Ingredients

100 g split green gram dal

250 g jaggery

400 ml coconut milk (150 ml first milk and 250 ml second milk)

4–5 green cardamoms, powdered or crushed

2 tablespoons ghee

6–8 cashew nuts, broken

8–10 raisins

Nutritional Value

(Per medium bowl or 4–6 tablespoons)

Calories: 200–250 kcal

Fat: 5–7 g

Fibre: A small amount of dietary fibre

Carbohydrates: 30–40 g

Sugar: 10–20 g (depends on the amount of jaggery used)

Protein: 3–5 g

Sodium: Negligible

Instructions

1. Wash the split green gram (moong dal) thoroughly under running water.
2. In a dry pan, roast the dal on low heat until it turns golden-brown and gives off a nutty aroma. Stir constantly to ensure even roasting. This can take 5–7 minutes. Once done, set it aside to cool.
3. Grate or crush the jaggery. Dissolve the grated or chopped jaggery in a little water in a pan over medium heat. Strain the jaggery syrup to remove any impurities. Keep it aside.
4. In a separate pan, add the roasted dal and enough water to cover it. Cook the dal until it becomes soft. This may take 10–15 minutes. You may need to add more water as it cooks. Once done, mash the cooked dal and set it aside.
5. In a large, heavy-bottomed pan, combine the cooked dal and the jaggery syrup. Mix well and cook on low heat for a few minutes, allowing the flavours to blend. Stir occasionally.
6. Reduce the heat to the lowest setting and slowly pour in the coconut milk while stirring continuously. Let it simmer for a few more minutes. (If using fresh milk, add the second milk at this stage. Simmer for 5–10 minutes and then add the first milk and let it simmer for a few minutes.)
7. Add the crushed or powdered cardamom to the payasam and mix it in.
8. In a separate small pan, heat the ghee. Add the cashew nuts and raisins and fry them until they turn golden-brown. Make sure not to burn them. Strain the fried cashews and raisins from the ghee and add them to the parippu payasam.
9. Parippu payasam can be served warm or at room temperature.

Slivers of fresh coconut browned in ghee can be used as garnish.

Chakka Pradhaman

Jackfruit, Jaggery and Coconut Milk Dessert

Jackfruit's versatility in both ripe and unripe forms makes it a staple ingredient in various Kerala dishes. While a halwa is one of the sweet dishes made with ripe jackfruit, it is also used in a pradhaman instead of ada or parippu.

Prep Time	**Cook Time**	**Serves**
5–10 minutes	30–40 minutes	4–6

Ingredients

250 g jackfruit pods, without seeds

250 g jaggery

400 ml coconut milk

4–5 green cardamoms, powdered or crushed

2 tablespoons ghee

6–8 cashew nuts, broken

8–10 raisins

Nutritional Value

(Per medium bowl or 4–6 tablespoons)

Calories: 200–250 kcal

Fat: 5–7 g

Carbohydrates: 30–40 g

Fibre: A small amount of dietary fibre

Sugar: 10–20 g (depends on the amount of jaggery used and the sweetness of the ripe jackfruit)

Protein: 3–5 g

Sodium: Negligible

Instructions

1. If using fresh jackfruit, remove the seeds and chop the ripe flesh into small pieces. You can also use canned, chopped jackfruit, which is already prepared.
2. Grate or crush the jaggery.
3. Heat the grated or chopped jaggery with a little water in a saucepan until it dissolves. Strain the jaggery syrup to remove any impurities. Keep it aside.
4. In a separate pan, add the jackfruit pieces and a little water. Cook them until they become soft and can be mashed easily. If you are using fresh coconut milk, you can use the thin milk here.
5. In a large, heavy-bottomed pan, combine the cooked jackfruit (along with the coconut milk if you have used the second fresh milk) and the jaggery syrup. Mix well and cook on low heat for a few minutes, allowing the flavours to blend. Stir occasionally.
6. Reduce the heat to the lowest setting and slowly pour in the coconut milk while stirring continuously. Let it simmer for a few more minutes. (If you are using fresh coconut milk, use the first milk and be careful not to let it boil vigorously as it can curdle.)
7. Add the crushed or powdered cardamom to the pradhaman and mix it in.
8. In a separate small pan, heat the ghee. Add the cashew nuts and raisins and fry them until they turn golden-brown. Make sure not to burn them. Remove the fried cashews and raisins from the ghee and add them to the chakka pradhaman.
9. Chakka pradhaman can be served warm or at room temperature.

Slivers of fresh coconut browned in ghee can be used to garnish.

Pazham Pradhaman

Banana, Jaggery and Coconut Milk Dessert

Like jackfruit, bananas, both ripe and unripe, are used in numerous dishes in Kerala. Ripe banana desserts are quite popular, particularly fritters. Banana can also be used in a pradhaman instead of jackfruit.

Prep Time

5–10 minutes

Cook Time

30–40 minutes

Serves

4–6

Ingredients

2–3 ripe bananas (preferably the Kerala variety)

250 g jaggery

400 ml coconut milk

4–5 green cardamoms, powdered or crushed

2 tablespoons ghee

6–8 cashew nuts, broken

8–10 raisins

Nutritional Value

(Per medium bowl or 4–6 tablespoons)

Calories: 200–250 kcal

Fat: 5–7 g

Carbohydrates: 30–40 g

Fibre: A small amount of dietary fibre

Sugar: 10–20 g (depends on the amount of jaggery used and the sweetness of the ripe bananas)

Protein: 3–5 g

Sodium: Negligible

Instructions

1. Peel the ripe bananas and mash them into a rough paste. Set aside.
2. Grate or crush the jaggery.
3. Heat the grated or chopped jaggery with a little water in a saucepan until it dissolves. Strain the jaggery syrup to remove any impurities. Keep it aside.
4. In a separate pan, add the banana and a little water. Cook for a few minutes. If you are using fresh coconut milk, you can use the thin milk here instead of water.
5. In a large, heavy-bottomed pan, combine the cooked banana (with the coconut milk if you have used the thin milk) and the jaggery syrup. Mix well and cook on low heat for a few minutes, allowing the flavours to blend. Stir occasionally.
6. Reduce the heat to the lowest setting and slowly pour in the coconut milk while stirring continuously. Let it simmer for a few more minutes. If you are using fresh coconut milk, use the first milk and be careful not to let it boil vigorously as it can curdle.
7. Add the crushed or powdered cardamom to the pradhaman and mix.
8. In a separate small pan, heat the ghee. Add the cashew nuts and raisins and fry them until they turn golden-brown. Make sure not to burn them. Remove the fried cashews and raisins from the ghee and add them to the banana pradhaman.
9. Banana pradhaman can be served warm or at room temperature.

Slivers of fresh coconut browned in ghee can be used as garnish.

Pal Payasam

Rice and Milk Dessert

This is one of the most popular and common payasams served at festivities and celebrations in Kerala. It has been my favourite since childhood, especially when it is cold, that little bit extra sweet and slightly thick in consistency.

Prep Time

10–15 minutes

Cook Time

15–20 minutes

Serves

4–6

Ingredients

100 g raw rice (preferably short-grained)

1 litre full-cream milk

200 g sugar

4–5 green cardamoms

2 tablespoons ghee

6–8 cashew nuts, broken

8–10 raisins

Nutritional Value

(Per serving of ½ cup or 4–6 tablespoons)

Calories: 150–200 kcal

Fat: 3–5 g

Carbohydrates: 30–40 g

Fibre: A small amount of dietary fibre

Sugar: 20–25 g (depends on the amount of sugar used)

Protein: 3–5 g

Sodium: Negligible

Instructions

1. Wash the rice thoroughly under running water until the water runs clear. Then soak it in enough water for about 30 minutes. Drain the water before using.
2. In a heavy-bottomed pan add the milk and rice. Bring to a boil. Lower the flame. Let the milk and rice mixture simmer on low heat. Keep stirring frequently to prevent the rice from sticking to the bottom. Cook until the rice is fully cooked and incorporated into the milk and the mixture thickens (reduces by ¼ or more). This can take 30–40 minutes.
3. Add the sugar to the mixture and continue to simmer on low heat. Stir well until the sugar dissolves completely. Then add the crushed or powdered cardamom. Stir well to combine.
4. In a separate small pan, heat the ghee. Add the cashew nuts and raisins, and fry them until they turn golden-brown. Make sure not to burn them. Remove the fried cashews and raisins from the ghee and add them to the pal payasam.
5. Allow the pal payasam to simmer for a few more minutes.
6. Keep stirring occasionally.
7. Once the pal payasam reaches your desired consistency (it thickens as it cools), remove it from heat. It can be served warm or chilled, according to your preference.

Slivers of fresh coconut browned in ghee can be used as garnish.

Nei Payasam

Rice and Jaggery Pudding

This is one of those payasams that do is not 'run' on the leaf, given its thicker consistency. I would make this payasam in my early cooking days, following a recipe from one of those pressure cooker recipe books. The result was not very encouraging as the rice, when mixed with the jaggery, became slightly hard grains. It is important that the rice is cooked very well otherwise the texture and feel will not be right, especially if you use long-grain rice. You want the payasam to be more than rice mixed with jaggery.

Prep Time	**Cook Time**	**Serves**
5–10 minutes	30–40 minutes	4–6

Ingredients

150 g raw rice
(preferably short-grained)
250 g jaggery
125 g ghee
6–8 cashew nuts
10–12 raisins
4–5 cardamoms
1 litre water

Nutritional Value

(Per single serving of 2 tablespoons)

Calories: 350–400 kcal
Fat: 15–20 g
Carbohydrates: 50–60 g
Fibre: 1–2 g
Sugar: 25–30 g
Protein: 4–6 g
Sodium: 50–100 mg

Instructions

1. Grate the jaggery or break into small pieces. Keep aside.
2. Peel the cardamom and crush the seeds into a coarse powder. Keep aside.
3. Wash the raw rice thoroughly under running water. Cook it with 2 cups of water in a heavy-bottomed pan or pressure cooker until it is soft and mushy. If using a pressure cooker, cook for 3–4 whistles.
4. While the rice is cooking, take another pan and add the jaggery with 2 tablespoons water.
5. Heat the jaggery on low heat, stirring continuously until it completely dissolves to form a syrup. Strain the syrup to remove impurities and set it aside.
6. Once the rice is cooked, mash it to achieve a coarse consistency.
7. In the same pan with mashed rice, add the jaggery syrup and mix well. Cook on low heat, stirring continuously to avoid lumps.
8. Add the cardamom powder to the payasam and mix well. Continue to simmer until it thickens further.
9. In a tempering pan, heat ghee. Add cashews and raisins and fry until they turn golden-brown. Make sure not to burn them. Remove the fried cashews and raisins from the ghee and add them to the nei payasam.
10. Once the nei payasam reaches the desired consistency, remove it from the heat. It will thicken slightly upon cooling.
11. Serve the nei payasam warm or at room temperature.

OTHER SADHYA DESSERTS

Apart from payasams, there are several other desserts and sweets that are commonly served as part of an Onam sadhya. While pieces of steamed nendran bananas (Kerala bananas) are considered essential, others like unniyappam, ela ada and pazham pori are added to make the sadhya more elaborate and so much more difficult to finish. These desserts could also be served as a teatime snack during festivities.

Unniyappam

Sweet Rice Flour Dumplings

While unniyappam is more commonly associated with festivals like Vishu, it is often served during Onam as well. These small, deep-fried rice, banana and jaggery dumplings have a unique taste and texture. A special pan, an appa chetti (with small, round moulds) is required to make it.

Prep Time

Overnight for rice, and a few hours for the fermentation

Cook Time

15–20 minutes

Makes

20–24 pieces

Ingredients

200 g raw rice

100 g jaggery, crushed or grated

2 ripe bananas (preferably the Kerala variety)

50 g coconut, fresh

¼ teaspoon cardamom powder

1 pinch salt

¼ teaspoon baking soda

Ghee or oil for frying

Nutritional Value

(For 1 medium-sized unniyappam)

Calories: 80–100 kcal

Fat: 2–4 g

Carbohydrates: 15–20 g

Fibre: 1–2 g

Sugar: 8–12 g

Protein: 1–2 g

Sodium: 20–30 mg

Instructions

1. Wash the raw rice. Soak it in water for about 4–6 hours or overnight.
2. Peel and chop or mash the ripe bananas.
3. In a pan, melt the grated jaggery with a little water to make a syrup. Strain the syrup to remove impurities.
4. Cut the coconut into small slivers, fry them in a pan with ghee or oil till they become slightly brown. Keep aside.
5. Drain the water and grind the rice, along with the chopped or mashed bananas to a semi-fine, slightly grainy batter using little or no water.
6. Add the fried coconut pieces, cardamom powder and jaggery syrup to the batter. Mix well to form a thick, smooth, pourable batter.
7. Allow the batter to ferment for 4–6 hours or overnight. This step is crucial for the appams to be soft.
8. Just before making the appams, add baking soda to the batter and mix well.
9. Heat the appa chetti and add a little ghee or oil to each mould.
10. Pour the batter into each mould, filling them up to 3/4th.
11. Cover the pan and cook on low to medium flame.
12. Once the edges start turning golden-brown, flip each appam using a skewer or a fork.
13. Cook the other side until it becomes golden-brown and crispy.
14. Once both sides are cooked, remove the appams from the pan and place them on a plate lined with a paper towel to absorb excess oil.
15. Repeat the process for the remaining batter.
16. Serve the unniyappams warm. They can be stored for a day or two in an airtight container.

Ela Ada

Steamed Pancakes

These are sweet, steamed pancakes made within folded banana leaf pieces, filled with a mixture of jaggery and grated coconut and covered with rice flour.

Prep Time

3–6 hours

Cook Time

15–20 minutes

Serves

12–15

Ingredients

For the outer covering (rice dough)

200 g raw rice

1 pinch salt

For the filling

150 g jaggery, crushed or grated

100 g coconut, grated

½ teaspoon cardamom powder

Banana leaves (for wrapping and steaming)

Ghee or coconut oil (for greasing)

Nutritional Value

(Per ela ada)

Calories: 150–200 kcal

Fat: 2–4 g

Carbohydrates: 30–40 g

Fibre: 2–3 g

Sugar: 10–15 g

Protein: 1–2 g

Sodium: 20–30 mg

You could use rice flour instead of soaking and grinding the rice. If you do not have an appa chetti, drop tablespoons full of the batter into hot oil and fry till golden-brown. You will not get uniform shapes, though.

Instructions

1. Wash the raw rice and soak it in water for 2–3 hours.
2. Drain the soaked rice and grind it into a smooth batter, adding a pinch of salt. Add water gradually to achieve a dosa-batter-like consistency.
3. Heat the rice batter in a pan. Keep stirring the batter over low heat till it forms a thick, dough-like consistency. Allow it to cool.
4. In a separate pan, melt the grated jaggery with a little water over low heat to make a syrup. Strain the syrup to remove impurities.
5. In a bowl, mix the grated coconut, jaggery syrup and cardamom powder. Ensure the mixture is well-combined and thick in consistency (add more grated coconut if required). Keep aside.
6. Cut banana leaves into squares or round pieces of 6–8 inches.
7. Lightly heat the banana leaves over a flame or in a pan to make them soft and flexible.
8. Grease the banana leaves with ghee or coconut oil.
9. Take a portion, around 2 tablespoons, of the rice dough and spread it evenly on a banana leaf to form a thin, circular layer.
10. Place and spread a portion of the filling in the centre of the rice dough. Leave a one-inch border.
11. Carefully fold the banana leaf to cover the filling, creating a semi-circle or rectangle. Seal the edges by pressing them together.
12. Place these in a steamer and steam for 15–20 minutes until the rice dough is cooked and has a translucent appearance.
13. Allow to cool slightly before serving.

Pazham Pori

Banana Fritters

While not exclusively a sweet, these banana fritters are a popular snack during Onam. Pieces of ripe bananas are coated in a sweet batter and deep-fried to golden perfection.

Prep Time	**Cook Time**	**Serves**
10–15 minutes	30 minutes	4–6

Ingredients

250 g or 2–3 medium-sized ripe bananas (preferably the Kerala variety)

125 g all-purpose

flour (maida)

25–30 g rice flour

25–30 g sugar

1 pinch salt

½ teaspoon baking soda

½ teaspoon turmeric powder (optional, for colour)

Nutritional Value

(Per pazham pori)

Calories: 150 kcal

Fat: 6–10 g

Carbohydrates: 25 g

Fibre: 3 g

Sugar: 14 g

Protein: 1 g

Sodium: 50–100 mg (depends on the amount of salt used)

Instructions

1. Peel the bananas and cut them into vertical halves or quarters, depending on the size. Make sure they are evenly sized for even cooking.
2. In a mixing bowl, combine the all-purpose flour, rice flour, sugar, salt, baking soda, and turmeric powder (if using).
3. Gradually add water and whisk the ingredients to form a smooth, lump-free batter. The consistency should be thick enough to coat the banana slices.
4. Heat oil in a deep pan or kadai over medium heat. Make sure it is hot.
5. Dip each banana slice into the batter, ensuring they are well-coated. Allow any excess batter to drip off.
6. Carefully place the coated banana slices in the hot oil, a few at a time. Fry until they turn golden-brown and crispy, turning them occasionally for even cooking.
7. Once they are golden-brown, use a slotted spoon to remove them from the oil. Place them on a plate lined with papevr towels to absorb any excess oil.
8. Repeat the dipping and frying process with the remaining banana slices and batter.
9. These can be served hot and crisp off heat or when cool later.

Adjust the quantity of sugar according to your taste preferences. You can also experiment with the batter consistency to achieve the desired texture. Remember to be cautious while frying and handle hot oil carefully.

Pazham Puzhungiyathu

Steamed Bananas

Ripe nendran/etha kaaya or Kerala bananas are steamed and served as an accompaniment at sadhyas. They can also make for a tasty evening snack. At times they are served along with puttu for breakfast.

Prep Time

3–6 hours

Cook Time

10 minutes

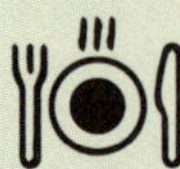

Serves

4–6

Ingredients

2–3 ripe bananas

Nutritional Value

(Per steamed banana)

Calories: 100 kcal

Fat: 0.5 g

Carbohydrates: 25 g

Fibre: 3 g

Sugar: 14 g

Protein: 1 g

Sodium: Negligible

Instructions

1. Cut the ripe bananas with skin horizontally into thick pieces of 5–7 cm.
2. Steam the banana slices until they are tender but still hold their shape. This usually takes 7–10 minutes.
3. These can be served immediately or stored for a couple of days in a refrigerator. If stored, warm them again in a microwave oven or steamer before serving.

APPENDIX 1

Substitutes for Vegan and Gluten-free Sadhyas

As mentioned earlier, it is entirely possible to have an Onam sadhya even if you are looking for a vegan or gluten-free spread. The ingredients that pose a problem in some of the recipes are curd, milk and maida.

Vegan Options

The rising popularity of veganism has led to a burgeoning market of plant-based alternatives to traditional dairy products. Among these alternatives, dairy-free curd options provide a versatile and delicious substitute for those seeking to adopt a plant-based lifestyle.

Soy Yogurt

One of the most widely embraced alternatives is soy yogurt. Crafted from soy milk and fermented with probiotics, soy yogurt mimics the creamy texture and mild tanginess of traditional dairy curd. It is a good option for dishes like avial and kaalan given its tanginess but is a bit overpowering when used for a cucumber pulissery.

Almond Yogurt

Almond yogurt offers another enticing option, prepared by fermenting almond milk with probiotics. It has a creamy texture with a nutty flavour and subtle tang. This could be suitable for inji thayir and cucumber pulissery.

Coconut Yogurt

Given the abundant use of coconut in various forms in a sadhya, coconut yogurt made from coconut milk is creamy with a thick consistency and a coconut-infused flavour profile that is a good vegan option for the curd-based dishes in an Onam sadhya.

Cashew Yogurt

Cashew yogurt, which also has a rich and creamy texture and is derived from fermenting cashew milk with probiotics, has a mild and slightly sweet taste. Like almond yogurt this could be suitable for inji thayir and cucumber pulissery.

Oats Yogurt

An increasingly popular option is oats yogurt, made by fermenting oats milk with probiotics. Given its smooth, slightly thick texture, its near-neutral taste makes it ideal as a dairy curd substitute. But for dishes like avial and kaalan you would need to add a tangy ingredient like aamchur for sourness which is essential for the dishes.

There are less common but possible alternatives in hemp curd, made from hemp milk, and flaxseed curd, made from flaxseed milk, but their distinct flavours are not entirely suitable for sadhya dishes.

So there are a number of possibilities to replace dairy products and still enjoy all the dishes in an Onam sadhya.

When it comes to dairy milk – used only in a few of the payasams – the alternatives are many. These can be bought from the store or made at home.

Soy Milk

Soy milk is an option for payasam given its creamy texture. To make soy milk at home, soak soybeans overnight, blend them with water and strain the mixture using a cheesecloth or a fine strainer.

Almond Milk

Almond milk with its mild, nutty flavour suits payasams well. It is available in stores but if you want to make it at home, soak almonds overnight and blend them with water. Strain well to remove solids and use.

Cashew Milk

Like almond milk, cashew milk with its creamy consistency and mild flavour is a good alternative for dairy-milk-based payasams. It can be made at home like almond milk.

Coconut Milk

Coconut milk is used in many of the payasams so use it as a substitute only if you are not serving a regular coconut-milk-based payasam.

Rice Milk

Rice milk is an interesting option, especially for payasams like pal payasam, which uses rice. It is also a good option for those with nut allergies. It has a thinner consistency than some of the other alternative milks. Rice milk is easy to make and has a mild taste. Blend cooked rice with water and strain.

A few of the other lesser-known and not very suitable milks are hemp milk and flaxseed milk.

When making these milk alternatives at home, it's essential to experiment with ratios to achieve the right consistency. Additionally, store-bought versions often come in different flavours. It is best to go for the unsweetened, plain ones.

When it comes to ghee, a dairy product, it is easy to replace it with the oil of your choice. If using oil, coconut oil is preferable.

Gluten-free Options

Maida or all-purpose flour is used in only one of the given recipes, pazham pori. There are some possible alternatives.

Rice Flour

Rice flour is already used in the recipe as it aids in achieving a certain crispness. If only rice flour is used, the pazham pori may become too crisp. It is preferable to mix it with any of the other flours mentioned below.

Corn Flour

Corn flour is the most common substitute and when mixed with rice flour, the pazham pori gets the desired crunchiness.

Almond Flour

Almond flour has a slightly grainy texture and is nutty and sweet. It is suitable for the pazham pori as bananas are dense in texture.

Coconut Flour

Coconut flour may be one of the better options as its coconut flavour adds to the pazham pori, plus it has a light, fluffy texture and absorbs a lot of liquid.

Other Flours

Oat flour is a bit coarse and has a mild oat flavour. Tapioca or cassava flour is neutral and adds a chewy texture. Another gluten-free option is chickpea flour, but it is not suitable given its dense and gritty texture.

APPENDIX 2

For those who would like to make coconut milk at home and keep a reserve of sambar and rasam powder.

COCONUT MILK

Coconut milk can be made at home with fresh coconut for those who do not want to use tinned or packaged coconut milk. While traditionally the coconut was squeezed by hand after being soaked in warm water, you could make use of a blender to make the process simpler.

When squeezed by hand the process is done twice. The first extract will be stronger, called the first milk, and the second, more diluted version is called the second milk. The second milk is used in the initial cooking process, instead of water, and the first milk is added at the end.

You could get two extracts with the blender too.

You must remember that homemade coconut milk tends to split when boiled for too long. This does not normally happen with packaged coconut milk. Fresh coconut milk contains proteins such as albumin which can coagulate under certain conditions, particularly when exposed to heat or acidic ingredients. When you boil fresh coconut milk, the heat can cause these proteins to alter their structure and coagulate, leading to curdling. On the other hand, packaged coconut milk often undergoes processing that can stabilise its proteins and emulsify the mixture, reducing the likelihood of curdling. Manufacturers may use various techniques such as homogenisation and adding stabilisers to achieve this. Additionally, some packaged coconut milk products may also contain additives or preservatives that help maintain their stability during cooking.

Ingredients

2 cups shredded coconut

3 to 4 cups (750 ml–1 litre) hot water

Instructions

1. Soak the coconut in 4 cups of hot but not boiling water for 5–10 minutes.
2. Transfer the soaked coconut and water into a blender. Blend on high speed for 2–3 minutes until the mixture is well combined and has a smooth consistency. (Or squeeze by hand.)
3. Strain the mixture through a cheesecloth or a fine strainer. Squeeze the coconut gathered in the cloth or strainer to extract as much milk as possible. The milk collected will be the first extract.

4. Add the strained coconut solids back into the blender. Add 1½ cups of hot water and blend for a couple of minutes.
5. Strain like before in a separate bowl. This would be the second milk which will be lighter and can be used to cook the ingredients, as per the recipe, in lieu of water.
6. You will get a yield of around 3 cups of the first milk and 1 cup of the second milk.

POWDERS

These powders for sambar and rasam can be made in bulk and used at any time, not just on Onam. They can be stored in airtight containers. There are dozens of recipes for these powders and each one claims to be authentic. The ones provided here come from my family, they have reached me after being passed from one generation to another, from great-grandmothers and grandmothers to mothers and aunts, modified perhaps at different stages. This is what the Chinnammus and Shangumans from my tharavad homes made on a regular basis.

SAMBAR POWDER

Ingredients

100 g coriander seeds

50 g cumin seeds

25 g black peppercorns

25 g fenugreek seeds

50 g mustard seeds

50 g chana dal

50 g urad dal

50 g dried red chillies

25 g turmeric powder

25 g asafoetida

6–8 sprigs curry leaves

Instructions

1. Start by dry roasting coriander seeds, cumin seeds, black peppercorns, fenugreek seeds, mustard seeds, chana dal, urad dal and dried red chillies separately in a pan over medium heat. Roast each ingredient until it becomes fragrant and slightly changes colour. Be cautious not to burn them as it can affect the taste.
2. Dry roast the curry leaves till they become crisp. Lightly dry roast the turmeric powder and asafoetida. Allow all the roasted ingredients to cool completely.
3. Grind the roasted ingredients together into a fine powder.
4. Let the sambar powder cool before storing in an airtight container. You will get around 500 g of sambar powder (2–2½ cups).

RASAM POWDER

Ingredients

100 g coriander seeds

50 g cumin seeds

25 g fenugreek seeds

50 g dried red chillies

25 g black peppercorns

50 g toor dal

50 g chana dal

6–8 sprigs curry leaves

Instructions

Start by dry roasting the coriander seeds, cumin seeds, fenugreek seeds, dried red chillies, black peppercorns, chana dal and urad dal separately in a pan over medium heat. Roast each ingredient until it becomes fragrant and slightly changes colour. Be cautious not to burn them as it can affect the taste.

1. Dry roast the curry leaves till they become crisp.
2. Allow all the roasted ingredients to cool completely.
3. Grind all the roasted ingredients together into a fine powder.
4. Let the rasam powder cool before storing it in an airtight container.
5. You will get around 400 g of rasam powder (around 2 cups).

It is advisable to use the coconut milk immediately. If required, it could be stored in a glass jar in the refrigerator for around two days.

Adjust the thickness of the coconut milk by varying the ratio of water to shredded coconut or by repeating the blending and straining process.

GLOSSARY

Adupu: A stove, traditionally wood-fired, made of clay, placed at ground level. These were common in old tharavad homes.

Chenda Melam: A traditional percussion ensemble performance featuring the chenda, a large, barrel-shaped drum that is played by striking the drumhead with sticks of varying thickness to achieve different musical notes. In addition to the chenda, other instruments like ilathalam (cymbals), chengila (gong) and elathalam (a small cymbal with a wooden base) are also included in the ensemble. During a Chenda Melam performance, the percussionists move in synchronised patterns.

Chingam: The first month of the Malayalam calendar. The Malayalam calendar is a lunar one, and Chingam usually corresponds to the months of August and September in the Gregorian calendar. The most significant festival during this month is Onam

Chomukha: A serving vessel with four bowls attached to a single handle, making it faster and easier for one person to serve multiple dishes.

Chundan Vallam: A traditional Kerala snake boat. These are long and narrow boats, a hundred feet or more in length, and can accommodate a large number of rowers, ranging from 64 to 128. The rowing style in snake boats involves rowers sitting in pairs and rowing to the rhythm of the Vanchipattu (boat song) sung by a leader. Snake boat races are a major attraction during Onam in Kerala. The Nehru Trophy Boat Race, held at the Punnamada Lake in Alappuzha, is one of the most famous such races.

Commis: In culinary terminology, a commis chef is a junior or apprentice chef, the entry level in a commercial kitchen.

Iruttukuthy Vallam: Also known as the 'Black Boat', it is another type of boat used in a snake boat race. Similar to the Chundan Vallam, it is long and narrow, and the crew row in a synchronised manner.

Kadai: A traditional Indian cooking vessel or wok. It is commonly used in Indian kitchens for various cooking purposes, including frying, sautéing and preparing a variety of dishes. A kadai can be made of different materials such as stainless steel, cast iron, aluminium or non-stick-coated materials. It is characterised by its deep, round shape with slightly flared sides. The depth allows for efficient frying and cooking. It comes in various sizes, allowing flexibility in cooking different quantities.

Kaikottikali: Also known as Thiruvathirakali, it is a traditional folk dance of Kerala, commonly performed by women during the festival of Thiruvathira, which typically falls in the Malayalam month of Dhanu (December–January). Thiruvathira is a festival associated with the worship of Lord Shiva. The participants wear traditional Kerala attire, which includes the white and gold Kasavu saree. The dance involves participants clapping hands while they move in a circular pattern. It is accompanied by traditional folk songs, often related to themes of love and devotion.

Karanavar: In the context of Kerala's traditional joint family system, the term 'Karanavar' refers to the eldest male member or the head of the family. The Karanavar holds a position of authority and responsibility within the family structure. In the traditional matrilineal system of Kerala, where lineage and inheritance are traced through the maternal line, the Karanavar is typically the senior male member of the maternal side.

Kasavu saree: A traditional handwoven saree from Kerala characterised by its distinctive off-white or cream-coloured fabric with a golden zari (metallic thread) border.

Kathakali: A classical dance-drama form in Kerala. It is highly stylised and known for its elaborate makeup, colourful costumes, intricate facial expressions and graceful body movements. Kathakali combines elements of dance, drama, music and ritual. The performances are traditionally based on classical Indian epics, particularly the Ramayana and the Mahabharata.

Kindi: A traditional water vessel or pitcher commonly used in households for pouring and storing water. Kindis have a distinctive shape, featuring a narrow neck and a wide base. The narrow neck allows for easy pouring of water, while the wide base provides stability. The spout of a kindi is designed for controlled pouring of water, making it convenient for various household tasks. It is also commonly used in temples.

Kolkali: A traditional folk dance in Kerala, typically performed in a circular formation, with the dancers moving around in circles. The most distinctive aspect of Kolkali is the use of sticks. The performers hold sticks in their hands and rhythmically strike them against those of their partners. Kolkali is accompanied by traditional folk songs.

Madhera: Same as Onathappan.

Mayilattam: A traditional dance form in Kerala. The term can be translated as 'peacock dance', where 'mayil' means peacock in Malayalam and 'attom' means dance. Performers wear costumes with peacock-feather designs or colours that resemble the plumage of a peacock. The dance is accompanied by traditional Kerala percussion instruments.

Mundu: A traditional garment worn by men and women in Kerala. It is essentially a piece of cloth draped around the waist. Its border has many colours. Some mundus with borders of thin and thick gold are worn on festive occasions.

Odi Vallam: They are smaller boats compared to Chundan Vallams and are often used for training purposes.

Onakazhcha: Gifts or offerings exchanged during Onam.

Onathappan: A traditional idol associated with Onam, it is typically a pyramid-shaped clay figurine that once represented Lord Vishnu but these days is associated with the demon king Mahabali and his return from the netherworld during Onam to visit his people. It is also called Madhera in some parts of Kerala.

Panchavadhyam: A traditional percussion ensemble performance in Kerala. The word 'panchavadhyam' literally means 'five instruments' in Sanskrit, and the ensemble typically includes a set of five different percussion instruments played by a group of five musicians.

Patalam: Also referred to as Patal Lok, it signifies the lowest realms or regions below the earth. In Hindu cosmology, the universe is often divided into different loks or worlds, and 'patal' is considered one of the lower realms.

Payasam: A traditional Indian dessert made by boiling milk, sugar/jaggery and rice/vermicelli or other similar ingredients.

Pookolam: A traditional floral art form that is a significant part of Onam celebrations in Kerala, which involves creating intricate and colourful floral arrangements on the ground. These flower carpets are made using a variety of vibrant flowers, leaves and petals arranged in beautiful patterns. Making a pookolam is generally a communal activity, with family members, neighbours and friends coming together to make elaborate and artistic floral carpets in front of their homes.

Pulikali: Also known as Kaduvakali, it is a traditional folk-art form in Kerala. The term 'pulikali' translates to 'play of the tiger'. Pulikali involves dancers who paint their bodies to resemble tigers and other wild cats. The theme revolves around hunting and the playful activities of a tiger.

Sadhya: A feast or banquet comprising many dishes served on a banana leaf at festivals and other celebrations.

Sutal Lok: In Hindu cosmology, Sutal Lok is one of the lower planes or realms (loks) in the cosmic hierarchy. It is considered a subterranean world. Sutal is described as a beautiful and opulent realm ruled by the benevolent demon king Bali (referred to as Mahabali and Maveli too). According to Hindu mythology, Bali was a virtuous and generous king who was granted the kingdom of Sutal by Lord Vishnu.

Swarg Lok: In Hindu cosmology, Swarg Lok refers to the celestial or heavenly realms. It is one of the higher planes of existence in the cosmic hierarchy. It is believed to be the abode of various deities, celestial beings and righteous souls who have performed good deeds in their earthly lives.

Tharavad: A traditional ancestral home or family house in Kerala, particularly among the Malayali community. The term is commonly used in the context of Kerala's joint family system. A tharavad typically represents a large house where several generations of a family live together, sharing common spaces and resources.

Theyyam: Also known as Theyyattam, it is a traditional dance and ritual art form of Kerala. The key features of the Theeyam dance are unique costumes, makeup and ornate headgear. Theeyam represents various deities, heroes and mythical characters from Hindu mythology and is normally performed within temple premises.

Uruli: A traditional shallow, wide-mouthed bowl or vessel commonly used in Kerala. These vessels are typically made of metal, such as bronze or bell metal. Urulis have a flat and wide shape with a shallow depth. They often feature a wide rim and a slightly curved or flat base.

Vallam Kali: Also known as Vallam Kettu, a traditional water sport or game that is part of Onam celebrations in Kerala. In Vallam Kali, teams of oarsmen paddle in a boat that can be quite long, with a narrow profile resembling a snake gliding through the water. Each boat typically accommodates a large number of oarsmen who row in unison to propel the boat forward.

Veppu Vallam: Traditional country boats that are also used in snake boat races. They are smaller in size compared to Chundan Vallams and have a more straightforward design.

Yagya: Yagya or Yagna are considered sacred acts of worship performed for various purposes, including seeking divine blessings, promoting prosperity and maintaining cosmic order.

ACKNOWLEDGEMENTS

Trident Cochin facilitated the food pictures. The manager Kirubhakaran opened up the hotel and kitchen to us, making sure the shooting went off smoothly. The Head Chef Rijo Thomas along with Chefs Afsalshabeeb, Nithil Johnson and Ajumal prepared the dishes just right, providing all the accompaniments that Dinesh wanted to enrich each frame, all this despite their strenuous schedules in the kitchen.

Arun Kapur has always backed my food and ventures and in this case has been more than generous in supporting the book.

Radha Thampuran, my maternal aunt, helped me with what my mother had started doing before she left us: refreshing memories of my childhood, helping me piece together scenes of how Onam was celebrated at the tharavads of my parents. Radha Thampuran also organised an Onam celebration at her home with the enthusiastic help of my cousins Latha, Devika and Jayshree. The three of them collected flowers, laid out a beautiful pookolam, went through the rituals and served a delicious sadhya. Latha, Devika and Jayshree spent their childhood in Kerala and were able to answer all my queries and filled in the blanks on how the festival was celebrated then and now.

Radha Thampuran was my 'Google aunt', all through the writing of the book I called her incessantly to clarify one doubt or the other. She also put me in touch with Sunil Thamban of Poornashri Catering who let us document his elaborate sadhya preparations during Onam.

Prema Viswanath, my sister, was my 'Google Maps'. She helped in navigating me to the right books and people for all the information I needed, especially Venugopal Paliath who was a font of information.

Rohit Srivastava went out of his way to help me with hotels in Kerala to support this book.

My niece Anita coordinated and put me in touch with a number of designers, including Mitu Das, the designer of this book.

Thank you, Madhavi Menon for connecting me with Devika J., who very patiently explained to me the socio-political significance of the festival and the changes that have taken place over the years.

Joemon of Kerala Expressions has always been my go-to person for any travel-related work in Kerala. He has never failed in guiding me to the right places and people. He never fails to provide me with resourceful drivers. This time it was Abdul Gafaar who made sure Dinesh and I were at the right places, at the right spot, to document all the Onam action. And through his vast network he was able to get me all the information required.

Archana and Janardan Pai were kind enough to take us to their ancestral home to photograph an old kitchen and traditional vessels.

Mimi Chowdhury is one person who always pushed and encouraged me to write a book on food.

Thanks to Krishan Chopra for giving me this opportunity and Mekhala Moorthy for being a very diligent editor seeing me through the entire process of writing and publishing.

This book would not have been possible without the enthusiastic involvement of Dinesh Khanna and his cameras. I am ever grateful to him for having instantly accepted the assignment.

And, of course, all this would not have been possible without the support, encouragement and guidance of my wife, Poonam Saxena. If not for her, this book may never have seen the light of day. And when it comes to the recipes and the food I cook there could be no better tasters and critics than her and our son, Arjun. So you can be sure the recipes here are tried and tested by the best!

ABOUT THE AUTHOR

Arun Kumar T.R. has had a fascinatingly varied career. He studied English literature from St. Stephen's College, Delhi University, then worked as a journalist and film critic for over eight years with the Times of India group.

His interest in films led him to becoming a filmmaker and he produced and directed several television serials, documentaries, corporate films, even a feature film. His work took him, among other places, to remote villages in Arunachal Pradesh, dense forests in Nagaland and the icy slopes of Everest Base Camp.

But all through these years, his passion for cooking, primarily South Indian coastal food, remained a constant. He is now a full-fledged chef, having headed a reputed brand and run a catering company for the past ten years. He launched the first food pop-up of Malayalee food in Delhi and went on to become brand chef for the popular coastal cuisine restaurant Zambar. Today, he's a chef-consultant for various clients.

Arun has won several awards, including multiple food awards instituted by the Times of India, the Best South Indian Chef award presented by the Indian Culinary Forum and the Top Chef Award for Excellence in South Indian / Coastal Cuisine by the Delhi Gourmet Club. He was also crowned Masterchef in a popular TV food show, *Pressure Cooker*.

From a Nair family, he has spent much time at his parents' ancestral tharavad homes in Kerala. He has watched Onam sadhyas being cooked in their traditional kitchens and later has cooked sadhyas himself, as well as coordinated and supervised innumerable Onam sadhya festivals at restaurants and caterings.

ABOUT THE PHOTOGRAPHER

Dinesh Khanna has been a freelance photographer for more than thirty years with an eclectic repertoire of commercial and personal work. He has been shooting food, people and interiors for advertising and corporate clients; he also does visual documentation for NGOs and social organisations. His personal work has been published as acclaimed books such as *Bazaar* and *Living Faith*. The books he has most recently worked on are *Right of the Line: The President's Bodyguard* and *Life in Rashtrapati Bhawan*. His work has been exhibited in solo and group shows in galleries from New Delhi to New York and Varanasi to San Francisco.

Dinesh is a managing trustee of Nazar Foundation and a co-founder of the Delhi Photo Festival. He was also a photography curator for the Serendipity Arts Festival. He has taught photography in various institutions such as Ashoka University; The One School, Goa; Jamia Millia Islamia, New Delhi; and MICA, Ahmedabad. He is a director at the Dhrish Academy of Photography in Musco Camera, where he conducts courses and workshops. He is also a visual consultant with Sahapedia.